Essential
Malaysia

by Neil Wilson

Neil Wilson is an experienced travel writer and photographer based in Edinburgh. He has travelled widely in Europe, North Africa, North America, Mexico, the Far East and Australia, and has written and photographed more than 20 guide books for various publishers, as well as contributing articles to magazines and newspapers.

AA Publishing

Written by Neil Wilson

Edited, designed and produced by AA Publishing.
© The Automobile Association 1998
Maps © The Automobile Association 1998
Reprinted May 1998

Distributed in the United Kingdom by AA Publishing,
Norfolk House, Priestley Road, Basingstoke,
Hampshire, RG24 9NY.

A CIP catalogue record for this book is available from
the British Library.

ISBN 0 7495 1631 3

The contents of this publication are believed correct at
the time of printing. Nevertheless, the publishers cannot
be held responsible for any errors or omissions or for
changes in the details given in this guide or for the
consequences of any reliance on the information provided
by the same. Assessments of attractions, hotels,
restaurants and so forth are based upon the author's own
experience and, therefore, descriptions given in this guide
necessarily contain an element of subjective opinion which
may not reflect the publisher's opinion or dictate a reader's
own experience on another occasion.

We have tried to ensure accuracy in this guide, but
things do change and we would be grateful if readers
would advise us of any inaccuracies they may encounter.

Published by AA Publishing, a trading name of Automobile
Association Developments Limited, whose registered
office is Norfolk House, Priestley Road, Basingstoke,
Hampshire, RG24 9NY.
Registered number 1878835.

Colour separation: BTB Digital Imaging, Whitchurch,
Hampshire

Printed and bound in Italy by Printers Trento srl

Above and page 5:
*traditionally dressed
figures*

Page 1: *residents of Bajau
stilt village, Semporna*

Page 5 (a): *Chinese
mansion in Georgetown*

Page15 (a): *Cameron
Highlands landscape*
15 (b): *packing tea*

Page 27 (a): *Wat
Chayamangkalaram*
27 (b): *Khoo Kongsi,
Georgetown*

Page 91 (a): *Pulau Kapas*
91 (b): *Khoo Kongsi*

Page 117: *travelling and
eating, Malaysia-style*

Find out more about
AA Publishing and the
wide range of services
the AA provides by
visiting our Web site at
www.theaa.co.uk

Contents

About this Book 4

About this Book

KEY TO SYMBOLS

➕ map reference to the maps found in the What to See section (see below)

✉ address or location

☎ telephone number

🕐 opening times

🍴 restaurant or café on premises or near by

Ⓔ nearest underground train station

🚌 nearest bus/tram route

🚉 nearest overground train station

🛳 ferry crossings and excursions by boat

✈ travel by air

ℹ tourist information

♿ facilities for visitors with disabilities

✋ admission charge

↔ other places of interest near by

❓ other practical information

▶ indicates the page where you will find a fuller description

---

Essential *Malaysia* is divided into five sections to cover the most important aspects of your visit to Malaysia.

Viewing Malaysia pages 5–14
An introduction to Malaysia by the author
   Malaysia's Features
   Essence of Malaysia
   The Shaping of Malaysia
   Peace and Quiet
   Malaysia's Famous

Top Ten pages 15–26
The author's choice of the Top Ten places to visit in Malaysia, with practical information

What to See pages 27–90
The four main areas of Malaysia, each with its own brief introduction and an alphabetical listing of the main attractions
   Practical information
   Snippets of 'Did You Know…' information
   3 suggested walks
   1 suggested tour
   2 features

Where To… pages 91–116
Detailed listings of the best places to eat, stay, shop, take the children and be entertained.

Practical Matters pages 117–124
A highly visual section containing essential travel information.

Maps
All map references are to the individual maps found in the What to See section of this guide.
For example, Kuching has the reference ➕ 82A1 – indicating the page on which the map is located and the grid square in which the island is to be found. A list of the maps that have been used in this travel guide can be found in the index.

Prices
Where appropriate, an indication of the cost of an establishment is given by **£** signs:
£££ denotes higher prices, **££** denotes average prices, while **£** denotes lower charges.

Star Ratings
Most of the places described in this book have been given a separate rating:

✪✪✪   Do not miss
✪✪   Highly recommended
✪   Worth seeing

Viewing
Malaysia

Neil Wilson's Malaysia

Light travel: a driver takes a brief rest in his trishaw in Kota Bharu

Muslim Malaysia
Islam was introduced to Malaysia by Muslim Indian traders in the 12th and 13th centuries, and has been the dominant force in the shaping of Malay culture. The Malaysian government promotes a religious, family-orientated society based on Islamic values, but the brand of Islam practised here is a relatively liberal one, far removed from the fundamentalism of Iran and Afghanistan.

An enduring feature of Malaysian public holidays is the phenomenon known as *kampung balik*. Meaning 'back to the village', it describes the great exodus of city dwellers as they head off to the countryside to visit family and friends, and spend a few days delighting in the simple pleasures of *kampung* life: fresh air, tasty food and companionship.

It is a good metaphor for Malaysia, an increasingly urbanised country that still manages to keep in touch with its rural origins. Malaysia is a young and ambitious nation – the government's long term plan, called Vision 2020, is to see Malaysia attain the status of a fully developed country by the year 2020. But among the skyscrapers of Kuala Lumpur, Johor Bahru and Georgetown, you can still find that keystone of Malaysian life, the open-air market, where office workers shop for fresh country vegetables and the latest music CDs, and the savoury smells of grilled *satay* and stir-fried noodles waft from the nearby hawker stalls. At weekends the same city dwellers like nothing better than to head for the nearest beach, lake or waterfall for a cooling bathe, or to pack a rucksack and set off for a hike in the forest.

For visitors, much of Malaysia's appeal lies in this combination of city and nature, where you can enjoy top quality hotels, restaurants and shopping along with the delights of beautiful beaches, unspoilt rain forest, exotic wildlife and spectacular coral islands.

Right: colour and bustle in Kota Bharu central market

6

Malaysia's Features

Geography
- Area: 329,758sq km (Peninsular Malaysia 131,689sq km; Sabah 73,620sq km; Sarawak 124,449sq km). East Malaysia and Peninsular Malaysia are separated by the South China Sea: the distance between Kuala Lumpur and Kota Kinabalu is about 1,600km.
- Highest peaks: Gunung Kinabalu (4,101m), Sabah; Gunung Tahan (2,187m), Pahang.
- Longest rivers: Sungai Rejang, Sarawak, 560km; Sungai Pahang, Pahang, 432km.
- Climate: equatorial. Hot, wet and humid all year round.

A typically busy street scene in Georgetown, Pulau Pinang

Temperatures average 25–30°C, with relative humidities of 82–86 per cent. Average rainfall: 2,500mm annually. The northeast monsoon (Nov to Mar) and the southwest monsoon (Jun to Oct) bring more wind and rain to the east and west coasts of Peninsular Malaysia respectively.

People and Society
- Population: 19.5 million (60.9 per cent Malay, 30.4 per cent Chinese, 8.2 per cent Indian, 0.5 per cent other).
- Religion: Muslim 52.9 per cent; Buddhist 17.3 per cent; Chinese folk-religion 11.6 per cent; Hindu 7.0 per cent; Christian 6.4 per cent; other 4.8 per cent.
- Languages: official language is Malay (known locally as Bahasa Melayu, or BM), but English is widely spoken. Other languages include Chinese (Mandarin, Cantonese, Hokkien, Hainan, Teochew), Tamil, Telegu, Punjabi, Hindi, Gujerati, Urdu, and numerous tribal dialects.
- Economy: manufacturing, palm oil, timber, rubber, tin, petroleum.

Government
Malaysia's government is a federal constitutional monarchy with two legislative houses, the Senate and the House of Representatives. There are 11 states in Peninsular Malaysia (Johor, Kedah, Kelantan, Melaka, Negeri Sembilan, Pahang, Perak, Perlis, Pulau Pinang, Selangor and Terengganu), plus the federal territory of Kuala Lumpur; and two states in East Malaysia (Sabah and Sarawak), plus the federal territory of Labuan. The government is led by the Prime Minister, while the sultans of the peninsular states take turns to act as Head of State.

Essence of Malaysia

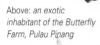

The attractions of Malaysia are many and varied, and if you have only a limited amount of time, you will need to be selective. If you are on a beach holiday, try to take in at least one city – either KL (Kuala Lumpur), Georgetown or Melaka. Don't miss the opportunity to walk through the jungle and delight in the colourful tropical birds and butterflies, and if possible, go snorkelling on a coral reef, and sample this magical undersea world at first hand.

Above: *an exotic inhabitant of the Butterfly Farm, Pulau Pinang*

Above: *shadow puppets in the National Museum, Kuala Lumpur*

Right: *a tranquil tropical idyll: the palm trees, deep blue sea and golden sands of Pulau Tioman*

THE **10** ESSENTIALS

If you only have a short time to visit Malaysia, or would like to get a really complete picture of the country, here are the essentials:

• **Wander the streets** of Chinatown in KL or Georgetown, and soak up the atmosphere of bustling commerce. Stop for a snack at a noodle stall.

• **Hire mask and fins** and go snorkelling on a coral reef. The variety of exotic marine life is breathtaking, from colourful corals, sea urchins, starfish and sea cucumbers to the multitude of rainbow-hued reef fishes.

• **Visit a Malay** *kampung* for an insight into the everyday lives of rural Malays.

• **Take a trip to one of Malaysia's hill resorts** (Cameron Highlands, Fraser's Hill, Maxwell Hill, Bukit Bendera), where you can escape the tropical heat while taking a stroll in the gardens or admiring the views.

• **Take a walk through the jungle** on one of the many hiking trails that can be found in Malaysia's national parks and local nature reserves.

• **Go shopping for souvenirs** amid the crowded stalls of a *pasar malam* (night market), and put your haggling skills to the test.

• **Attend a cultural show** for a brief taste of the colourful dances and traditional ceremonies that play an important part in Malay culture.

• **Take a boat trip to a deserted beach**, and relax amid the classical Malaysian combination of soft, white coral sand, sparkling turquoise waters and emerald jungle fringed with coconut palms.

• **Eat dinner at dusk** in a traditional outdoor hawker centre. Sample the traditional hawker dishes of *satay, nasi goreng, curry laksa, char kway teow* and Hainan chicken rice.

• **Visit KL's Golden Triangle** to experience the modern Malaysia of soaring skyscrapers, vast shopping malls, designer boutiques and bars and night clubs.

Above: *exploring the clear, blue waters off Sabah*

Top: *kite-flying, a popular pastime*

9

The Shaping of Malaysia

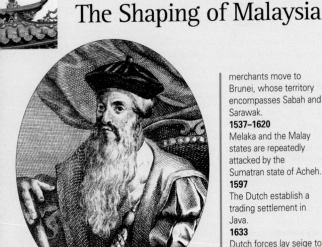

Above: *Alfonso de Albuquerque, the Portuguese invader who conquered Melaka*

38000 BC
Early humans inhabit the Niah Caves, Sarawak.

8000–6000 BC
The northern part of the Malay Peninsula is settled by Orang Asli ('original peoples') from the Andaman Islands in the Indian Ocean.

2nd century BC–7th century AD
Indian adventurers arrive in the Malay Peninsula, and found a series of small, independent Hindu states. Chinese trading vessels begin to venture into the Malay Archipelago.

7th–14th centuries AD
The great Hindu empire of Srivijaya occupies the shores of the Strait of Melaka, including eastern Sumatra and the western Malay Peninsula.

*c*1400
The Sumatran prince Parameswara founds the sultanate of Melaka.

15th century
Melaka develops into the most important commercial port in Southeast Asia, and becomes a centre for the spread of Islam throughout the Malay Peninsula and Archipelago. The sultanate of Melaka expands over most of the Malay Peninsula and eastern Sumatra.

1511
Melaka falls to a Portuguese invasion force led by Alfonso de Albuquerque, and becomes the main European trading port in the Far East. Muslim merchants move to Brunei, whose territory encompasses Sabah and Sarawak.

1537–1620
Melaka and the Malay states are repeatedly attacked by the Sumatran state of Acheh.

1597
The Dutch establish a trading settlement in Java.

1633
Dutch forces lay seige to Melaka.

1641
The Portuguese garrison at Melaka surrenders to the Dutch.

Late 17th century
Minangkabau immigrants from Sumatra settle in the area around Melaka; Buginese traders (from Sulawesi) establish sultanates in Selangor and Johor.

1762
The Sultan of Sulu gives Sabah to the British.

1786
Captain Francis Light acquires the island of Penang (Pinang) as a base for the British East India Company.

1795
Following the defeat of Holland in the Anglo-Dutch war of 1781–3, the British take over Melaka and other Dutch possessions in the Far East.

1826
Unification of Melaka,

Penang and Singapore under British administration as the Straits Settlements.

1841

The Sultan of Brunei makes James Brooke the 'White Rajah' of Sarawak, in return for his help in suppressing a rebellion.

1874

The Treaty of Pangkor marks the beginning of British political control in the Malay Peninsula.

1888

Sarawak and Sabah become British protectorates.

1896

Perak, Selangor, Negeri Sembilan and Pahang unite to form the Federated Malay States, with Kuala Lumpur as capital.

1914

Johor joins with Kedah, Perlis, Kelantan and Terengganu to form the Unfederated Malay States.

1941

Japanese invasion of the Malay Peninsula begins at Pantai Dasar Sabak, near Kota Bharu.

1946

Creation of United Malays National Organisation (UMNO) to promote political interests of Malays. Sabah and Sarawak become British crown colonies.

1948

All peninsular states, with the exception of Singapore, are united in the Federation of Malaya.

1948–60

'The Emergency': Malaysian Communist Party insurgents, opposed to British rule, wage a guerilla war, attacking rubber plantations and estates.

1957

Malaya achieves independence. The declaration is made at Dataran Merdeka in KL on 15 August. Tuanku Abdul Rahman is the first Prime Minister.

1963

Singapore, Sarawak and Sabah join Malaya to form the Federation of Malaysia.

1965

Singapore is separated from Malaysia, and becomes an independent republic.

1981

Dr Mahathir Mohammed, leader of UMNO, becomes Prime Minister; he is re-elected in 1995.

Below: *Sir Stamford Raffles bought Singapore for £13,500 in 1824*

11

Peace & Quiet

Hill Resorts

Malaysia's famous hill stations are a legacy of the colonial era, when perspiring British planters and administrators sought refuge from the tropical heat and humidity on the peaks of local hills. Maxwell Hill (➤ 47) and Bukit Bendera on Pulau Pinang (➤ 62) were cleared in the 19th century to provide a retreat for officials living in Taiping and Georgetown, and are still dotted with colonial bungalows surrounded by rose gardens and neatly trimmed lawns.

The more remote resorts of Fraser's Hill, 100km northeast of Kuala Lumpur (➤ 40), and the Cameron Highlands (➤ 40) were not cleared until the 1920s. Both were developed as hill stations, with cottages, gardens and golf courses, but the Cameron Highlands were also cultivated with extensive tea plantations and vegetable farms. Apart from the cooler climate, the main attractions of the hill resorts include walks and jungle-treks, bird-watching, horse-riding, superb views, and cream teas in

'Olde English' style hotels. The Genting Highlands resort near Kuala Lumpur (➤ 41) is a resolutely modern affair: a rash of concrete luxury hotels and theme parks built around the central attraction of Malaysia's only casino complex.

National Parks

One of Malaysia's main attractions is its magnificent wildlife. Forests cover over 70 per cent of the land area, although less than 50 per cent is untouched, primary rain forest; logging, agriculture and rubber and oil-palm plantations have taken their toll. Many national parks have been created to protect wildlife and scenery, while also allowing public access. The biggest is Taman Negara (➤ 26), covering an area of virgin forest six times the area of Singapore. There are forest trails around the park HQ, and the adventurous can attempt a nine-day round trip to the summit of Gunung Tahan and back. Other spectacular national parks include Niah (➤ 88), Gunung Mulu and Bako (➤ 87 and 88) in Sarawak; and Kinabalu (➤ 76) in Sabah.

Left: *Pulau Tioman provides a luxurious setting for a range of isolated beach resorts*

Beaches and Coral Islands

Beautiful tropical beaches are one of the main reasons for Malaysia's popularity with Western tourists. The best beaches are on the east coast of Peninsular Malaysia, especially on the offshore islands like Pulau Tioman (➤ 66) and Pulau Perhentian (➤ 56); on Pulau Langkawi and Pulau Pangkor (➤ 56) in the west; and in Sabah. The west coast mainland beaches and those on Pulau Pinang, though attractive, often suffer from murky waters because of muddy river outflows, occasional pollution, and the shallow waters and strong currents of the Strait of Melaka.

The best beaches of all are those on the coral-fringed islands off the east coast, and in the Tunku Abdul Rahman and Turtle Islands national parks in Sabah.

Malaysia's Famous

Dr Mahathir Mohamad

Malaysia's best-known political figure is the country's current (and longest serving) prime minister. Born the son of a teacher in Alor Setar in 1926, he worked as a doctor before entering politics and became prime minister in 1981 as the leader of UMNO (United Malays National Organisation). He has been returned overwhelmingly at every election since then. Now in his 70s, Dr Mohamad has announced that he will eventually stand down for his likely successor, deputy prime minister Anwar Ibrahim.

Malaysian royalty
Malaysia has no fewer than nine royal families, linked to the sultans of nine of the peninsular states – the sultans elect one of their number to act as *yang dipertuan agong* (the Malay equivalent of 'king' or 'head of state') for five years at a time. There are no *paparazzi* trailing Malaysia's royalty, however, as criticism of the sultans could lead to a charge of sedition.

Tuanku Abdul Rahman

The first prime minister of an independent Malaysia is remembered in street names in almost every Malaysian city. A British-educated lawyer, Abdul Rahman was born in 1903 and became president of UMNO in 1951, before successfully negotiating his country's independence. He served as prime minister from 1957 to 1970.

Perry Ramlee

The most famous name in Malaysian music is undoubtedly that of Perry Ramlee, who founded Malaysian pop music in the 1950s with his orchestral adaptations of traditional Malay melodies and romantic songs. A major street in Kuala Lumpur's Golden Triangle is named after him.

Lat

The work of Malaysia's most famous and best-loved artist can regularly be enjoyed in the pages of the national daily

Tuanku Abdul Rahman, being installed as the Paramount Ruler of Malaysia in 1957

newspaper, the *New Straits Times*. The cartoonist, though still only in his 40s, is a national institution, a shrewd commentator on the fads, failings and preoccupations of Malaysia's people and politicians. His keenly observed sketches neatly capture the contrasts between *kampung* and city life, and the many dilemmas of a traditional culture faced with explosive technological progress. Original Lat cartoons are collectors' items, and he has published several books of compilations.

Top Ten

1
Cameron Highlands

☩ 42B3

Tourist Information Centre

✉ Main Street, Tanah Rata

☎ (05) 491 1266

🕐 Mon–Fri 8–4:15, Sat 8–12:45. Closed Fri 12:15–2:45 and Sun

🍴 Many restaurants and hawker stalls in Tanah Rata and Berincang (£–££)

🚌 Regular bus service from Tapah (60km away on North-South Highway) and from Kuala Lumpur

♿ None

❓ Half-day guided tours can be booked at the Tourist Information Office in Tanah Rata

The rolling green acres of a tea plantation in the Cameron Highlands

Cradled among the mist-shrouded peaks of the Malaysian interior, this rural retreat offers a welcome respite from the tropical heat.

Sixty kilometres of steep, winding road lead from Tapah up to the cool and misty heights of the Cameron Highlands. This fertile fold in the forest-clad mountains of the Main Range, discovered in 1885 by the British surveyor William Cameron, lies 1,500m up, and has an average daily temperature of 22°C. It was developed as a hill station in the 1920s–'40s, with large tea-estates and small Chinese market-gardens. The cool climate attracted British colonials, and the farmers were joined by planters' bungalows, rose gardens, hotels and a golf course.

The main tourist centre is Tanah Rata, whose main street is lined with cheap Chinese hotels, cafés, shops and hawker stalls. Chalets, backpackers' hostels and more expensive hotels can be found on the fringes of town. About 2km beyond Tanah Rata is the Olde Smokehouse, a large mock-Tudor hotel built in 1937 which appears to have been transplanted straight from England, complete with oak-beam ceilings, log fires and a red telephone box.

One of the region's main attractions is the Sungai Palas Tea Estate, which offers guided tours of the tea-processing factory, where wood fires are still used in the curing process. Other sights include a rose garden, butterfly gardens and the Sam Poh Tong temple in Berincang, but the most rewarding activity is hiking along marked trails through the hills. The less energetic can drive to the 2,031m summit of Gunung Berincang, where a viewing tower offers a superb panorama (in clear weather).

2
Kinabalu National Park

A mysterious world of deep forests, tree-ferns and pitcher plants surrounds the rugged granite pinnacles of Southeast Asia's highest mountain.

The 4,101m peak of Mount Kinabalu dominates the skyline east of Kota Kinabalu in Sabah. (Its name derives from the belief of the local Kadazan people that the spirits of their ancestors inhabit the mountain: *aki nabalu* means 'revered place of the dead'.) This huge mass of granite was injected

into the Earth's crust some nine million years ago; since then erosion has removed the softer surrounding rocks to leave the ice-sculpted summit dome projecting above the tree-line. Its slopes support a bewildering variety of plant communities, which change gradually with increasing height. The area was declared a national park in 1964.

The park HQ has a visitors' centre, restaurants and accommodation. Hiking trails lead into the forest, ranging from one-hour strolls to the two-day ascent of Mount Kinabalu. The park's unusual flora includes almost 1,000 varieties of orchid, some growing in the Mountain Garden behind the visitors' centre. Most famous are the insectivorous pitcher plants (*Nepenthes*), which trap insects in a water-filled leaf. The largest, *Nepenthes rajah*, has been found holding over two litres of water and a drowned rat!

 75B2

 100km northeast of Kota Kinabalu

 (088) 211652 (Sabah Parks Office, Kota Kinabalu)

 Daily, 24 hours

 Restaurants at park HQ, and at Laban Rata on mountain (£)

 Bus or minibus from Kota Kinabalu to park entrance, 2-hour journey

 None

 Park entrance free; compulsory permit and guide for climbing mountain, moderate

 Poring Hot Springs (➤ 77)

Mount Kinabalu's granite peak soars above the lush lower slopes

 Guided walks on nature trails. The climb to the summit (8.5km, 2,200m of ascent) takes two days and, though hard work, is within the capabilities of most fit and healthy hikers. (Not recommended for those with heart trouble or high blood pressure.) You will need walking boots, waterproofs, warm clothing (including gloves and hat), water bottle, trail food and a torch.

3
Kuala Lumpur

🕇 42B2

**MATIC (Malaysia Tourist
Information Complex)**

✉ 109 Jalan Ampang,
50540 Kuala Lumpur

☎ (03) 264 3929

🕐 Daily 9–9

🍴 Restaurant serving
Malaysian specialities
(£££)

🚌 Bus 176 or 177 from
Lebuh Ampang, or
minibus 23 or 24 from
Jalan Hang Lekiu

♿ Few

✋ Free

❓ Audio-visual
presentation on
Malaysia (daily 10,
noon, 2:45 and 5). Live
performances of
traditional Malaysian
dancing (Tue, Thu, Sat
and Sun at 3:30)

*Kuala Lumpur's lively
Chinatown district*

*Malaysia's booming capital retains a core of
colonial elegance amid the chrome and glass of
modern shopping malls and skyscrapers.*

Look out of the window as you fly into Kuala Lumpur, and
your first impression will be of endless building sites. KL is
one of the fastest developing cities in the world, with vast
amounts of money being invested in new office buildings,
shopping centres, communications systems, and an
elevated light-rail transport (LRT) network.

But despite all this frantic activity, KL manages to hold
on to much of its historic appeal (▶ 31–9). The green
square of the Padang (now called Dataran Merdeka, or
Independence Square), the centre of the old, colonial city,
still preserves a certain tranquillity amid the hurly-burly of
traffic and towering skyscrapers, a feeling heightened by
the restrained elegance of the surrounding buildings: the
Royal Selangor Club, St Mary's Church, and the Moorish-
style façade of the Sultan Abdul Samad Building.

The history of the different ethnic communities that
contributed to KL's multicultural population is preserved in
a number of 19th-century mosques and temples, in the
streets of Chinatown and Little India, and in the exotic
flavours of the city's various cuisines. No visit would be
complete without a meal of *satay, ayam goreng,* or *char
kway teow* at one of the many traditional hawker centres.

The modern city's attractions include bargain-hunting in
the Golden Triangle's air-conditioned shopping malls, and
strolling through the greenery of the lovely Lake Gardens.

4
Kuching

The former seat of the 'white rajahs' lazes along the banks of the Sarawak River, an intriguing and easy-going blend of British and Bornean influences.

Kuching was founded in 1839 by the British adventurer James Brooke, who was made Rajah of Sarawak by the Sultan of Brunei in return for his assistance in quelling a tribal uprising. The town expanded during the 'golden age' of Brooke's nephew and successor, Charles (1868–1917), who oversaw the building of a palace (the Istana) for himself and his wife, Ranee Margaret (1870); a Court House (1874); Fort Margherita and the Square Tower (1879); and the grand Sarawak Museum (1891). Charles' eldest son, Vyner Brooke, was the last of the white rajahs (1917–46); Sarawak was taken by the Japanese in 1941, and became a British Crown Colony after the war, before joining the Federation of Malaysia in 1963.

✚ 82A1

Tourist Information Centre

✉ Padang Merdeka, Kuching

☎ (082) 410944

🕐 Mon–Thu 8–4:15, Fri 8–4:45, Sat 8–12:45. Closed Sun

🍽 None

♿ None

✋ Free

Kuching today is an attractive mixture of old and new (► 84–5, 86). The waterfront, which has recently been renovated, overlooks the swirling brown waters of the Sarawak River, and is a pleasant place to stroll, with views across the river to the Brooke-era buildings of Fort Margherita and the Istana. Behind the waterfront there is a lively Chinatown, with several fascinating antique shops and some excellent food stalls. The green square of the Padang was the heart of the 19th-century city, and is still bordered by the elegant façades of the Court House, the Post Office and the famous Sarawak Museum, one of the best museums in Southeast Asia.

Kuching is also a good centre from which to explore southwestern Sarawak. Local travel agents can arrange river safaris which include visits to Iban longhouses in the interior, or trips to the wildlife sanctuaries of Semenggoh, Bako and Gunung Gading.

A stall-holder points out a bargain at Kuching's Jalan Satok market

5
Melaka

43C1

Melaka Tourist Information Centre

✉ Jalan Kota, Melaka

☎ (06) 283 6538

🕐 Daily 8:45–5. Closed Fri 12:15–2:45

❓ Sound and Light Show nightly at 9.30, at the Padang

Open to the skies: the hilltop church of St Paul's in Melaka

History lingers along the banks of the Melaka River, once the most important trading harbour in the Malay Archipelago.

Legend claims that in 1400 an exiled Sumatran prince, Parameswara, founded a town on the site of a *melaka* tree, where he had witnessed a mouse deer attack one of his hunting dogs. The town had a fine natural harbour on the main sea route between India and China, and it quickly developed into a prosperous commercial port frequented by Indian, Persian, Arabian and Chinese merchants. At its height, the Sultanate of Melaka controlled the whole Malay Peninsula and much of Sumatra, and was responsible for spreading Islam throughout the region.

But Melaka's wealth attracted the attention of Portuguese traders, and the city fell to Alfonso d'Albuquerque in 1511. During the 16th century Melaka grew into the most important *entrepôt* in Southeast Asia, and was eventually taken by the Dutch in 1641, before finally passing into British control in the 1820s. With the silting of Melaka's harbour and the increasing importance of Singapore, the town gradually declined into a sleepy backwater, and remained that way until its re-birth as a tourist destination. Each of Melaka's various rulers has left his particular mark in his turn, and the long and cosmopolitan history makes it one of the most fascinating cities in Malaysia.

Melaka's attractions include the charming hilltop church of St Paul's; the ruined 16th-century gateway to the Portuguese fort of A Famosa; the 17th-century Dutch Stadthuys (Town Hall); the distinctive Melakan mosques with their Sumatran-influenced architecture; and the beautiful Peranakan town houses (▶ 49–52). Melaka is also famed for its crafts and antique shops, many of them clustered along Jonkers Street (now called Jalan Hang Jebat) in Chinatown.

6
Niah National Park

The awe-inspiring limestone caverns of Niah,
their walls daubed with primitive paintings, have
provided shelter for humans for 40,000 years.

Bones discovered in the Niah Caves in the 1950s prove that *Homo sapiens* was living here 40,000 years ago, the oldest evidence of human habitation yet found in Southeast Asia. The caves were first described to Europeans by the British naturalist Alfred Russell Wallace in 1864, but archaeological excavations did not begin until

 83C2

✉ 110km south of Miri, Sarawak

☎ (085) 436637 (National Parks Office, Miri): phone in advance to check that caves are open

🍴 Cafeteria at park HQ (£)

1954, when the caves were bought by the Sarawak Museum. The diggings uncovered Stone Age tools and a man's skeleton dated to 38,000 BC: there were also cave paintings and 'boat burials' (graves in which canoes were used as coffins) thought to be 1,000 to 2,000 years old.

Niah and the surrounding forest were made a national park in 1975, and a trip to the caves is unforgettable. A raised plank-walk leads from the park HQ to the caves, through jungle where you can see macaques, hornbills, bulbuls, trogons and butterflies; you might also spot flying lizards, water monitors and mouse deer. The Great Cave at Niah is over 90m high and 180m wide, and is inhabited by millions of bats and swiftlets, whose twilight comings and goings provide an impressive spectacle. The plank-walk continues into the darkness (bring a torch) and along a passage to the Painted Cave, where prehistoric paintings adorn the walls. Accommodation is available at park HQ: book at the Tourist Information Centre in Miri (▶ 88) or Kuching (▶ 19, 84–5).

🚌 Bus (2 hours) from Miri to Batu Niah, then boat or taxi (5 minutes) to park HQ

♿ None

✋ Free; boat and accommodation: moderate

↔ Gunung Mulu National Park (▶ 88)

❓ Organised tours from Kuching and Miri. Chalet and hostel accommodation available; book at the Visitors' Information Centre in Miri or Kuching

7
Pulau Langkawi

42A5

Tourist Information Centre

Jalan Persiaran Putra, Kuah

☎ (04) 966 7789

🕓 Daily 9–1, 2–6

🚢 Express ferries to Pulau Langkawi run hourly 8–6 from Kuala Kedah and Kuala Perlis. Crossing time 1–1½ hours.

✈ There are daily flights to Langkawi from Kuala Lumpur and Pinang. For details contact MAS ☎ (03) 746 3000 or Pelangi Air ☎ (03) 746 5524

Right: *the spectacular Telaga Tujuh waterfall*

Once the haunt of fishermen and pirates, Pulau Langkawi now attracts tourists with its white-sand beaches, limestone peaks and waterfalls.

Pulau Langkawi lies 30km off the coast of northwestern Malaysia, surrounded by an archipelago of over 100 uninhabited islands. The main island is 30km long and 16km wide, and has an international airport, luxurious resort hotels, two new golf courses and gleaming new shopping centres taking advantage of the island's duty-free status. The main town of Kuah is small but busy, with little of interest. The main focus for tourists is the beach strip of Pantai Cenang and Pantai Tengah on the west coast, where golden sands are lined with restaurants and hotels, and watersports facilities are available. Good beaches can also be found at Pantai Kok, Tanjung Rhu, and Datai.

Less than an hour's walk from Pantai Kok is the waterfall of Telaga Tujuh (Seven Wells), where a stream cascades 100m through seven shallow pools, bordered by lush forest. There are other scenic waterfalls at Temurun, near Datai, and Durian Perangin, 15km north of Kuah.

Coral-fringed islands dot the waters around the coast. Boat trips visit Pulau Dayang Bunting, with its freshwater lake, and the wildlife sanctuary of Pulau Singa Besar. Pulau Payar, 30km south, is a marine park where you can dive, snorkel or view the coral reef from glass-bottomed boats.

Above: *discovering the beautiful surroundings of Pulau Langkawi by boat*

8
Pulau Pinang (Penang)

42A4

Tourist Information Centre

3rd floor concourse, Komtar Shopping Centre, Jalan Pinang, Georgetown

(04) 261 4461

Mon–Sat 10–6, Sun 11–7

Penang Tourist Association

Jalan Tun Syed Sheh Barakbah, Georgetown (behind Fort Cornwallis)

(04) 261 6663

Mon–Thu 8:30–1, 2–4:30, Sat 8:30–1

Railway station in Butterworth on mainland

A 24-hour ferry service operates between Butterworth and Georgetown

Pinang is connected to the mainland by a 13.5km bridge. A toll is charged when crossing to the island, but not on the return trip

With beautiful beaches, a fascinating Chinatown, historic buildings, stilted fishing villages and a hill resort, Pulau Pinang is Malaysia in microcosm.

The island of Pinang lies off the west coast of Malaysia, at the northern end of the Strait of Melaka (➤ 57). It was acquired in 1786 by Captain Francis Light as a base for the East India Company, and thus became the British Empire's first foothold in the Far East. Captain Light built a stronghold at Fort Cornwallis on the easternmost point of the island, and supposedly encouraged settlers to clear the surrounding jungle by firing a cannon-load of coins into the bush.

The newly established city of Georgetown boomed for a few decades, but was soon eclipsed by the rising importance of its southern counterpart, Singapore, founded by Sir Thomas Stamford Raffles in 1819. Chinese traders flocked to Georgetown and made their fortunes from tin, rubber and copra, building opulent mansions along 'Millionaire's Row' (Jalan Sultan Ahmad Shah).

Industry has been concentrated on the east coast between the harbour and the airport, while tourist development has taken place chiefly in Georgetown and along the north coast beaches at Batu Feringgi and Teluk Bahang.

Georgetown is a large, modern city, but it has retained a genuinely fascinating Chinatown, with a truly Chinese character that has been lost in KL and Singapore. Relics of the city's colonial past include the crumbling remains of Fort Cornwallis, the fine buildings around the Padang, the lush delights of the Botanical Gardens, and the cool retreat of Bukit Bendera (Pinang Hill). Away from the city, the island's many attractions include fine beaches, fishing villages, jungle hiking trails and colourful temples.

Colourful lanterns decorate the 19th-century temple of Kek Lok Si, Pulau Pinang

9
Pulau Tioman

Limpid, turquoise waters, gently waving palm trees and soft sands make Tioman the quintessence of a tropical island paradise.

Pulau Tioman is the largest and best-known of the many islands that lie off Malaysia's east coast. It was for centuries used as an anchorage and watering stop for ships trading between China and the Malay Archipelago (its twin 1,000m peaks are visible from a great distance), and it gained fame in the 1950s as the 'Bali Hai' of the Hollywood musical *South Pacific*. Its beautiful beaches and pristine waters have since drawn increasing numbers of tourists, who can choose from a wide range of accommodation, ranging from humble wooden beach huts to world-class luxury resorts.

Tioman's large size (38km by 19km) means that it has been able to absorb a considerable amount of development without losing its 'desert island' appeal, and there are plenty of remote beaches and islets where it is still possible to enjoy an afternoon of solitude. The only real village is at Kampung Tekek on the west coast, close to the main jetty and the airport, where there are shops, money-changers and public telephones. There is a short stretch of road on the west side, and a rough track leading from Tekek across to the superb sandy bay of Kampung Juara, but most places are best reached by boat.

The main reason for visiting Tioman is simply to enjoy the beautiful beaches, and perhaps go snorkelling on the nearby coral reefs; the best beaches are at Juara, Bunut, Nipah and Teluk Salang. Other activities on offer include scuba-diving, jungle-trekking (the island is rich in wildlife), horse-riding, windsurfing, canoeing, sailing and fishing.

A tranquil scene: the serenity of Pulau Tioman

✚ 43D2

Tourist Information Centre

✉ Jalan Abu Bakar, Mersing (no tourist office on Tioman)

☎ (07) 799 5212

🕐 Daily 8–12:45, 2–4:20. Closed Fri PM

🍴 Resort hotels and chalet developments have their own restaurants (£–££)

⛴ Daily ferry services from Mersing (▶ 53). Crossing takes 4 hours by regular boat, 1½ hours by hydrofoil. Departure times depend on tide

✈ Pelangi Air has regular flights to Tioman from Kuala Lumpur, Kuantan and Singapore ☎ (03) 262 4448

10
Taman Negara

✛ 43C3

✉ Park HQ reached via a 59km riverboat trip from the jetty at Kuala Tembeling (a 4-hour drive from Kuala Lumpur). Kuala Tembeling can also be reached by train from Kota Bharu, Johor Bahru and Singapore.

☎ (03) 905 2872 (National Parks Department, Kuala Lumpur); (03) 264 3929 (Malaysia Tourist Information Centre, Kuala Lumpur); (09) 266 3500 (Taman Negara Resort for accommodation)

🍴 Restaurant at Taman Negara Resort (£–££)

✋ Cheap; camera permit: cheap; fishing permit: cheap

❓ Organised tours from Kuala Lumpur, two to four days

A water buffalo, at home in the vast sanctuary of Taman Negara

The green heart of Peninsular Malaysia is a sanctuary for threatened wildlife, including elephant, rhinoceros, tiger, leopard, buffalo and tapir.

Taman Negara (the name means simply 'national park') encompasses 4,343sq km of tropical rain forest, an area more than six times the size of Singapore. Established in 1938 (when it was called the King George V National Park), it lies on the north side of the Tembeling River and includes the peak of Gunung Tahan (2,187m), the highest summit in Peninsular Malaysia.

A diverse range of habitats and plant communities exists within the park boundaries, from the dense, evergreen forests of the lowlands, characterised by tall tropical hardwoods draped in thick, creeping lianas, through the more open montane forests of oak, laurel and native conifers, to the high-level (over 1,500m) cloud forests of Gunung Tahan, where the slopes support a bizarre growth of gnarled rhododendrons, giant heather, tree-ferns, and dwarf oaks draped in mosses, ferns, orchids and pitcher plants.

Don't expect to see rare species such as tiger, leopard, sun bear, rhinoceros or elephant on a flying visit; however, a night spent at one of the park hides, overlooking a salt-lick, can result in an encounter with wild ox, wild boar, tapir, and various species of deer; primates such as macaques, leaf monkeys and gibbons are more often heard than seen in the dense vegetation. More easily seen are the 250 species of birds that inhabit the park, including spectacular varieties like the giant argus pheasant, hornbills, trogons, pittas, eagles, and kingfishers.

A network of hiking trails radiates from the park HQ to various camps, hides, caves and peaks. Treks range in length from a few hours to a nine-day round-trip to the summit of Gunung Tahan.

What To See

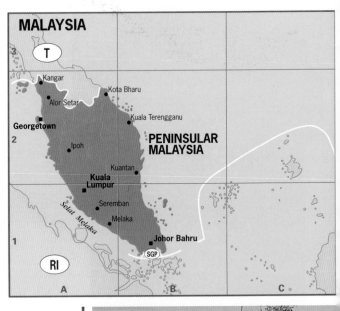

MALAYSIA

T

Kangar
Kota Bharu
Alor Setar
Kuala Terengganu
Georgetown
PENINSULAR
MALAYSIA
Ipoh
Kuantan
Kuala
Lumpur
Selat Melaka
Seremban
Melaka
Johor Bahru
RI
SGP

A   B   C

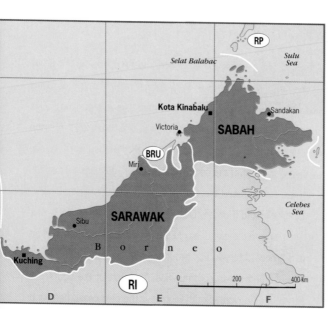

Boats moored up in the waters off Pulau Langkawi

Peninsular Malaysia

Malaysia is divided into two parts by the South China Sea. Peninsular (West) Malaysia occupies the tip of the Southeast Asian mainland, while the two states of Sabah and Sarawak (East Malaysia) lie in the northern part of the island of Borneo. Peninsular Malaysia, home to most of the country's population, contains the capital, Kuala Lumpur, and the tourist destinations of Melaka, Pinang, Langkawi and Tioman. Development is concentrated in the west, where the centuries-old shipping route through the Strait of Malacca (Melaka) has brought trade, industry and thriving Chinese and Indian communities. This part of the country is served by the North–South Highway. The east coast, heartland of traditional Malay culture, has superb beaches at Kampung Marang and on the offshore islands of Pulau Tioman, Pulau Redang and Pulau Perhentian; and, in the mountainous, jungle-clad interior, the wildlife paradise of Taman Negara.

'I see it now – the wide sweep of the bay, the sands, the wealth of green infinite and varied, the sea blue like the sea of a dream…'

JOSEPH CONRAD
Youth (1902)

Kuala Lumpur

Kuala Lumpur, usually shortened to KL, is a sprawling city of 1.3 million people – the commercial, industrial and political capital of modern Malaysia. First impressions are of gleaming skyscrapers, concrete freeways and countless building sites, but the city has managed to preserve many fascinating aspects of its history.

*Kuala Lumpur's
Parliament House*

Kuala Lumpur has come a long way since it was founded by Chinese tin prospectors in 1857. The miners' settlement at the meeting of the Kelang and Gombak rivers (*'kuala lumpur'* means 'muddy confluence') grew rapidly in the 1880s following the construction of a railway link with the port of Kelang, and its central location led to its selection in 1895 as the capital of the Federated Malay States. Grand colonial government buildings were raised on the west side of the river, while wealthy merchants and rubber planters built their mansions along Jalan Ampang on the east bank. Cricket is still played on the green field of the Padang, overlooked by the Moorish façade of the Sultan Abdul Samad Building and the mock-Tudor of the Royal Selangor Club. Across the river lies KL's Chinatown, with its bustling street markets and colourful temples, and on the neck of land where the Kelang and Gombak meet is the Masjid Jame (Friday Mosque), built in 1897.

The city's other attractions include the Lake Gardens, which contain a Bird Park, a Butterfly Park, and Orchid and Hibiscus Gardens; the cultural collections of the National Museum; and the glitzy shopping malls of the Golden Triangle, the commercial hub of modern KL (► 18).

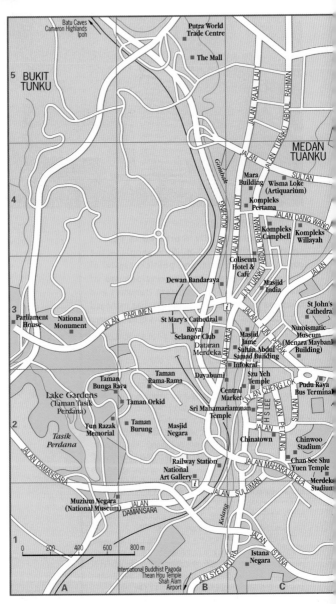

Batu Caves
Cameron Highlands
Ipoh

Putra World
Trade Centre

■ The Mall

5 BUKIT
TUNKU

MEDAN
TUANKU

JALAN SULTAN

Mara
Building
Wisma Loke
(Artiquarium)

Kompleks
Pertama

4

JALAN DANG WANGI

Kompleks
Campbell

Kompleks
Willayah

Coliseum
Hotel &
Café

Dewan Bandaraya

Masjid
India

3 Parliament
House

National
Monument

JALAN PARLIMEN

St Mary's Cathedral

Royal
Selangor Club

Dataran
Merdeka

Masjid
Jame

Sultan Abdul
Samad Building

Infokraf

St John's
Cathedra

Numismatic
Museum
(Menara Maybank
Building)

Taman
Bunga Raya

Taman
Rama-Rama

Dayabumi

Szu Yeh
Temple

Pudu Raya
Bus Terminal

Lake Gardens
(Taman Tasik
Perdana)

Taman Orkid

Central
Market

Sri Mahamariamman
Temple

Tun Razak
Memorial

Taman
Burung

Masjid
Negara

Chinatown

Chinwoo
Stadium

2

Tasik
Perdana

JALAN DAMANSARA

Railway Station

National
Art Gallery

JALAN MAHARAJALELA

Chan See Shu
Yuen Temple

Merdeka
Stadium

Muzium Negara
(National Museum)

JALAN
DAMANSARA

JALAN SULAIMAN

1

0   200   400   600   800 m

Istana
Negara

International Buddhist Pagoda
Thean Hou Temple
Shah Alam
Airport

JLN SYED PUTRA

JALAN ISTANA

A   **B**   **C**

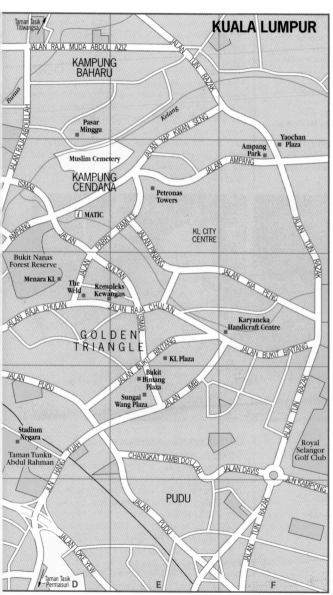

KUALA LUMPUR

Taman Tasik Titiwangsa

JALAN RAJA MUDA ABDUL AZIZ

JALAN TUN RAZAK

KAMPUNG BAHARU

Batu

Kelang

JALAN RAJA ABDULLAH

Pasar Minggu

JALAN YAP KWAN SENG

Yaochan Plaza

Ampang Park

ISMAIL

Muslim Cemetery

JALAN AMPANG

KAMPUNG CENDANA

Petronas Towers

AMPANG

i MATIC

JALAN

PARRY

JALAN RAMLEE

JALAN PINANG

KL CITY CENTRE

JALAN TUN RAZAK

Bukit Nanas Forest Reserve

JALAN SULTAN

JALAN KIA PENG

Menara KL

The Weld

Kompleks Kewangan

JALAN RAJA CHULAN

ISMAIL

JALAN RAJA CHULAN

Karyaneka Handicraft Centre

G O L D E N   T R I A N G L E

JALAN BUKIT BINTANG

JALAN BUKIT BINTANG

KL Plaza

JALAN PUDU

Bukit Bintang Plaza

JALAN IMBI

Sungai Wang Plaza

Stadium Negara

JALAN TUAH

Taman Tunku Abdul Rahman

CHANGKAT TAMBI DOLLAH

JALAN TUN RAZAK

Royal Selangor Golf Club

JALAN DAVIS

JLN KAMPONG

JALAN HANG

PUDU

JALAN PUDU

JALAN OKE YEW

JALAN TUN RAZAK

Taman Tasik Permaisuri

D

E

F

What to See in the City Centre

CENTRAL MARKET ⭐⭐

This Art Deco building on the east bank of the Kelang river was built in the 1930s as the city's meat and vegetable market, but has since been converted to a lively collection of shops, restaurants and handicraft stalls. It is connected by a walkway to the Dayabumi complex, across the river. Cultural shows are performed here every evening.

➕ 32C2
✉ Jalan Hang Kasturi
☎ (03) 274 6542
🕐 Daily 10–10
🍴 Restaurants, stalls (£)
🚌 Near major bus terminal
↔ Chinatown, Dataran Merdeka (► below)

CHINATOWN ⭐⭐⭐

Although the Chinese population is now spread throughout the city, this district of ancient two-storey shophouses east of Central Market retains the bustling commercial atmosphere of old KL, especially in the teeming *pasar malam* (night market) on Jalan Petaling, where the pavements are jammed with stalls selling leather goods, watches, clothing, cassettes and CDs, souvenirs and bric-à-brac, and the aromas of Chinese cooking waft from the crowded noodle restaurants.

➕ 32C2
🍴 Hawker stalls (£)
🚌 Near major bus terminals
♿ None
↔ Central Market (► above)

Opposite page: *the Masjid Jame (Friday Mosque)*
Below: *a street stall in KL's Chinatown*

DATARAN MERDEKA (INDEPENDENCE SQUARE) ⭐⭐

Formerly known as the Padang (Malay for 'field'), this wide expanse of vivid green turf marks the heart of old Kuala Lumpur. It is surrounded by reminders of the city's colonial past: the ornate Sultan Abdul Samad Building (► 37); the mock-Tudor premises of the Royal Selangor Club, focal point of KL's high society since the 1890s; the white spire of St Mary's Cathedral, built in 1894; and the Memorial Library, housed in a grand old 1909 office building.

A plaque of black marble set in the turf marks the spot where the Union Jack was run down at midnight on 31 August 1957, and replaced with the Malayan flag, as the country proclaimed its independence (*merdeka*).

➕ 32B3
✉ Jalan Raja
🍴 In Dayabumi Shopping Centre
♿ None
🎟 Free
↔ Masjid Jame (see below), Sultan Abdul Samad Building (► 37)

GOLDEN TRIANGLE ☺☺☺
This is the name given to the recently developed area east of the Kelang river, a glitzy district of high-rise offices, 5-star hotels, up-market shopping malls, nightclubs and restaurants, dominated by the twin steel-and-glass spires of the Petronas Towers. These 88-storey, 452m-tall towers are the world's tallest buildings, and form the focal point of KL City Centre, the city's flagship commercial development.

MASJID JAME (FRIDAY MOSQUE) ☺☺☺
The prettiest of Kuala Lumpur's mosques was built in 1909 to the design of British architect AB Hubbock, who drew inspiration from the Mogul mosques of northern India. The building is a delicate confection of colonnades, onion domes and minarets, made of red-and-white brick and set on the neck of land at the confluence of the Klang and Gombak rivers.

MASJID NEGARA (NATIONAL MOSQUE) ☺
A 73m-tall minaret marks the site of Malaysia's National Mosque, a celebration of Islam in white marble with fountains set amid landscaped gardens. Built in the 1960s, the mosque can accommodate up to 8,000 worshippers beneath its 18-pointed umbrella dome (symbolising the 13 states of Malaysia plus the Five Pillars of Islam).

MENARA KL (KL TOWER) ☺
This telecommunications tower sits atop Bukit Nanas (Pineapple Hill) overlooking the Golden Triangle (see above), and is a distinctive landmark on the city skyline. At 421m it is the third highest in the world, and the revolving restaurant and viewing galleries at the top provide a magnificent panorama of the city.

- 33D3
- ✉ Jalan Sultan Ismail, between, Jalan Ampang and Jalan Imbi
- 🍴 Hawker stalls (£)
- 🚌 Bus 15
- ↔ Menara KL (▶ below)

- 32C3
- ✉ Jalan Tun Perak
- 🕐 Sat–Thu 9–12:45, 2:30–4:15. Closed Fri
- LRT Masjid Jame
- 🎫 Free
- ↔ Dataran Merdeka (▶ above)
- ❓ Dress suitably (▶ 70–1)

- 32B2
- ✉ Jalan Sultan Hishamuddin
- 🕐 Sat–Thu 9–6, Fri 2:45–6
- 🎫 Free
- ❓ Dress suitably (▶ 70); robes are provided for visitors wearing shorts or skirts

---

- 33D3
- ✉ Jalan Puncak
- ☎ (03) 208 5448
- 🕐 Daily 10–8
- 🍴 Seri Angkasa (£££)
- 🎫 Moderate
- ↔ Golden Triangle (▶ above)

35

+ 32A1
✉ Jalan Damansara
☎ (03) 282 6255
🕐 Daily 9–6 (closed for Hari
   Raya holiday)
🍴 Stalls in grounds
🚌 Minibus 33, 35 or 38
♿ Few
💷 Cheap (under 12s free)
↔ Taman Tasik Perdona
   (➤ 38)

+ 32B2
✉ Jalan Sultan Hishamuddin
🍴 Restaurant and snack
   bars
🚌 Minibus 33, 35 or 38
↔ Masjid Negara (➤ 35)

MUZIUM NEGARA (NATIONAL MUSEUM) ✪✪

The imposing National Museum building dates from 1963, and reflects various aspects of the traditional architecture of wooden Malay houses. The rather dry displays cover local history and culture, traditional arts and crafts, weapons, currency, and Malaysian wildlife. Transport exhibits in the grounds around the museum include traditional boats, a Penang Hill funicular railway car, a Scottish-built aircraft, a fire engine, vintage cars, and one of the first Proton Saga cars to be built in Malaysia.

RAILWAY STATION ✪✪

Kuala Lumpur's main line railway station is a tourist attraction in its own right, an architectural fantasy designed by AB Hubbock and built in 1910. It is a magnificent concoction of Moorish spires and minarets, keyhole arches and cupolas, complemented by the equally ornate façade of the Malayan Railways Administration Building, across the road.

+ 32C2
✉ Jalan Tun H. S. Lee
🕐 Early–late
🚌 Near major bus terminals
♿ None
💷 Free
↔ Chinatown (➤ 34)

*An impressive introduction
to the city: KL's ornate
railway station*

SRI MAHAMARIAMMAN TEMPLE ✪✪✪

A back street in Chinatown conceals the magnificent *gopuram* of the Sri Mahamariamman Temple, a tiered tower of multi-coloured ceramic tiles and ornate sculptures that surmounts the entrance to one of Malaysia's oldest Hindu temples. The temple was founded in 1873 on the site of the railway station, and was moved to this spot in 1885. It contains shrines devoted to the gods Shiva and Ganesh, and a silver chariot dedicated to the Lord Muruga that takes part in the annual procession from the temple to the Batu Caves (➤ 40) during the Thaipusam festival (➤ 116).

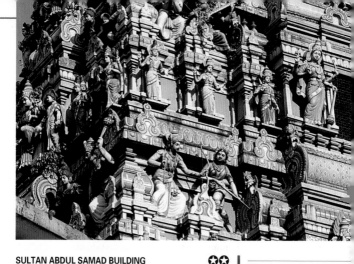

SULTAN ABDUL SAMAD BUILDING ✪✪

The clock-tower of the Sultan Abdul Samad Building, affectionately known as 'Big Ben', is one of KL's most familiar landmarks. The building, with its ornate Moorish façade of pink brickwork, white stucco, keyhole arches and copper-domed towers, was designed by the British architect AC Norman (who also designed St Mary's Cathedral) in the 1890s, and was once the home of colonial government offices. It has recently been renovated, and now houses the Malaysian Supreme Court and the High Courts.

SZU YEH TEMPLE ✪✪

Tucked away down an alley is one of Kuala Lumpur's oldest Chinese temples, built in the 1880s. The construction of the tiny temple was completed with the aid of Yap Ah Loy, the first 'Kapitan China' (head of the Chinese community) in Kuala Lumpur. A century of incense smoke has darkened the red and gold decoration inside the temple, where a photograph of Yap Ah Loy can be seen on an altar near the back.

TAMAN BURUNG (BIRD PARK) ✪✪

A small, landscaped valley on the eastern edge of the Lake Gardens has been enclosed and stocked with a wide variety of Southeast Asian bird species. Footpaths and board-walks lead among forest glades and miniature waterfalls.

TAMAN ORKID AND TAMAN BUNGA RAYA ✪
(ORCHID AND HIBISCUS GARDENS)

Across the road from the Bird Park, set on a rounded hilltop, is KL's Orchid Garden. Over 800 species of Malaysian orchids are grown in the beds and pergolas laid out among ornamental ponds and walkways. A path at the far side leads into the neighbouring Hibiscus Garden, which contains 500 varieties of Malaysia's national flower.

🔢 32C3
✉ Jalan Raja
🕐 Not open to the public

Above: intricate decoration and fascinating sculptures on Sri Mahamariamman Temple

🔢 32C2
✉ Lorong Bandar, off Lebuh Pudu
🕐 Early–late
🚌 Near major bus terminals
♿ None
💵 Free
↔ Central Market, Chinatown (▶ 34)

🔢 32B2
✉ Jalan Cenderawasih
🕐 Daily 9–5
🍴 Drinks and snacks
🚌 Tourist shuttle bus
💵 Cheap
↔ Taman Orkid (▶ below)

🔢 32B2/32A2
✉ Jalan Cenderawasih
🕐 Daily 9–6.30
🚌 Tourist shuttle bus
💵 Mon–Fri free; Sat–Sun cheap
↔ Taman Burung (▶ above)
❓ Orchid Bazaar, weekends

37

🔢 32B2
✉️ Jalan Cenderasari
☎️ (03) 293 4799
🕐 Daily 9–5 (6 on weekends and holidays)
🍴 Restaurant
🚌 Tourist shuttle bus
💵 Moderate

TAMAN RAMA-RAMA (BUTTERFLY PARK)

This enclosed garden contains over 100 species of colourful Malaysian butterflies, which can be seen at close quarters as they feed on trays spread with hibiscus blossom. The most spectacular is the Rajah Brooke's Birdwing, which has long, tapered black wings with an iridescent stripe of emerald green. The neighbouring museum has displays of butterflies, moths, giant millipedes, scorpions and other exotic insects from all over Southeast Asia.

🔢 32A2
✉️ Main entrance on Jalan Parlimen; also accessible by tunnel from grounds of National Museum
🕐 Dawn–dusk
🍴 None
🚌 Tourist shuttle bus
💵 Free
🔁 Muzium Negara (➤ 36), Taman Burung, Taman Orkid (➤ 37)

TAMAN TASIK PERDANA (LAKE GARDENS) ⭐⭐⭐

These 90-hectare gardens, set on wooded hills around an artificial lake, were laid out in the 1880s, and are still a favourite weekend retreat for weary city-dwellers. There are several kilometres of shady walks, and at weekends you can rent rowing boats on the lake. Across Jalan Parlimen, at the northern end of the gardens, is the National Monument, which commemorates those who died in the war against Communist insurgents during the Emergency (1948–60). It was unveiled in 1966, and is the work of Felix de Weldon, who also created the USA's Iwo Jima Monument in Washington DC.

Taman Tasik Perdana (Lake Gardens)

🔢 Off map 32B1
✉️ Off Jalan Syed Putra
🕐 Daily 9–6
🍴 Hawker stalls (£)
🚌 Minibus 27
💵 Free
❓ Lion dances and Chinese opera during Chinese New Year festivities

THEAN HOU TEMPLE ⭐

This huge, modern temple, brightly decorated in red and gold, sits on a hilltop a few kilometres south of the city centre. It is dedicated to the goddess of mercy, Kuan Yin, and is a popular venue for Chinese weddings. The temple and pagoda share the site with a 100-year-old Buddhist shrine and a sacred Bodhi tree (the Buddha is said to have achieved enlightenment while sleeping beneath a Bodhi tree). The hilltop setting offers good views over the city.

A Walk Around Kuala Lumpur

This walk takes in many of KL's main landmarks and includes a stroll through busy Chinatown

From the LRT station visit the Masjid Jame (▶ 35), then return and head left along Jalan Tun Perak, beneath the raised LRT track. Turn left at Jalan Tuanku Abdul Rahman, along the colonnaded front of the Dewan Bandaraya (City Hall). Immediately after crossing the bridge over the Gombak River turn left along the river bank.

This tree-lined street passes behind the law courts and offers good views across the river to the Masjid Jame.

Turn left across the next bridge, then take the second street on the right (Jalan Hang Kasturi), which leads to Central Market (▶ 34). Continue along the pedestrian precinct beyond the market and turn left along Jalan Cheng Lock.

This takes you into the bustling heart of Chinatown (▶ 34), where you can enjoy browsing among shops and stalls.

Cross the busy street and take the second street on the right, Jalan Petaling. Follow it for two blocks, then turn right on Jalan Sultan, and right again along Jalan Tun HS Lee.

The walk now leads past the impressive Sri Mahamariamman Temple (▶ 36).

At the next junction turn left on Jalan Hang Lekir to emerge at a busy intersection where you turn right along Jalan Hang Kasturi to return towards Central Market. Cross the footbridge over the river that leads left from the pedestrian precinct, then turn right along the river bank on the far side. At the next bridge turn left past the Infokraf Handicraft Centre, and cross busy Jalan Raja to the south end of Dataran Merdeka.

Join the bargain-hunters in Chinatown on your way around Kuala Lumpur

Distance
3km

Time
1 hour, excluding time spent visiting attractions

Start point
✚ 32C3
Masjid Jame LRT station

End point
Dataran Merdeka (Independence Square)
✚ 3BB3

Lunch
Riverbank Restaurant (£)
✉ Ground Floor (Unit G14), Central Market
☎ (03) 274 6652

What to See in Peninsular Malaysia

ALOR SETAR

New development is changing the face of Alor Setar, the charming capital of Kedah state. Gleaming new shopping malls and a modernistic telecommunications tower have sprung up around the old square and its historic buildings. The graceful, black domes and elegant minarets of the Masjid Zahir, dating from 1912, face the ornate wooden palace of the 19th-century Balai Besar, still used for royal ceremonies. The **Muzium DiRaja** (Royal Museum) houses several colourful miniature tableaux of Malay customs and a collection of boats once used by the sultans of Kedah.

AYER KEROH

Concentrated along the road leading from the North–South Highway to Melaka are several outdoor attractions, including a Butterfly Farm, a Crocodile Farm, a boating lake, an aquarium, and the Melaka Zoo. The Mini ASEAN and Mini Malaysia parks have wooden houses built in the styles of the six ASEAN countries (Malaysia, Singapore, Thailand, Indonesia, Brunei and the Philippines) and the 13 states of Malaysia, each with displays of arts and crafts.

BATU CAVES

Concealed within a towering limestone outcrop, these huge cathedral-like caves were discovered by an American naturalist in 1878. A flight of 272 steps leads to the Temple Cave, whose 100m tall chamber has been used as a Hindu temple for over 100 years. The caves are the focus of the annual Thaipusam festival (► 116), when up to 800,000 people celebrate here. A cave at the foot of the outcrop, 'the Art Gallery', contains Hindu wall paintings and statues.

CAMERON HIGHLANDS (► 16, TOP TEN)

DESARU

This 20km beach of golden sand near the southern tip of Peninsular Malaysia is lined with luxury resorts and golf courses, and is aimed mainly at wealthy weekenders from Singapore and Johor Bahru.

FRASER'S HILL (BUKIT FRASER)

Named after Louis James Fraser, a 19th-century tin prospector, Fraser's Hill nestles amid the forested highlands at a cool altitude of 1,500m. The area was first developed as a hill station in the 1920s, and it still retains a colonial air, with its neat lawns and rose gardens, 9-hole

---

42A4
Muzium DiRaja
✉ Lebuhraya Darulaman, 2km north of town centre
☎ (04) 733 1162
🕐 Daily 10–6. Closed Fri noon–2:30
♿ None
🖐 Free

42C1
🕐 All attractions open daily 9–6
🍴 Fast food and hawker stalls (£)
♿ None
🖐 Cheap; Forest Park: free

42B2
✉ 13km north of Kuala Lumpur city centre
🕐 Daily 7AM–9PM
🍴 Hawker stalls (£)
🚌 Bus 11, 70
♿ None
🖐 Temple Cave: free; Art Gallery: cheap
↔ Templer Park (► 69)
❓ Thaipusam festival (► 116)

43D1
🍴 Restaurants in beach resort hotels (££–£££)
🚌 Bus from Kota Tinggi (or taxi)

42B3
☎ (09) 362 2201
🍴 Wide range (£–££)
🚌 66 or 100 KL to Kuala Kubu Bahru, connecting bus (or taxi)

A daunting flight of steps sweeps up the cliff to the hidden Batu Caves

public golf course and cream teas at the Old Smokehouse Hotel. Activities include bird-watching, walking and bathing in the pool below the Jeriau Waterfall. Bungalows and chalets are available, and two large resort developments.

GENTING HIGHLANDS ⊗

Genting, from the Chinese for 'above the clouds', stands in stark contrast to other Malaysian hill resorts, its twinkling lights clearly visible from KL on a clear night. This is a brash, round-the-clock, casino resort, with a casino, 5-star hotels, a cable-car, a theme park, a boating lake, a 16-lane bowling alley, a heated indoor swimming pool and an international class 18-hole golf course.

IPOH ⊗⊗

The state of Perak (which means 'silver' in Malay) takes its name from the silvery tin ore for which it was once famous. Ipoh, the state capital, was built on the profits of the tin mines, and is today a pleasant city with many colonial reminders. The tree-lined *padang* (square) is overlooked by the mock-Tudor Royal Ipoh Club, and near by are the elegant façades of the City Hall and the Railway Station. Other attractions include the cave temple of Perak Tong, 6km north, and a **Geological Museum** with an exhibition on tin ore (take a taxi).

➕ 42B2
☎ Enquiries and reservations: (03) 262 2666
🍴 Restaurants in resort hotels (££–£££)
🚌 Regular bus service from Puduraya bus station, KL

➕ 42B3
Geological Museum
✉ Jalan Sultan Azlan Shah, 5km east of centre
☎ (05) 545 7644
🕐 Mon–Fri 8–4:15, Sat 8–12:45
✋ Free

Mosque in Kota Bharu

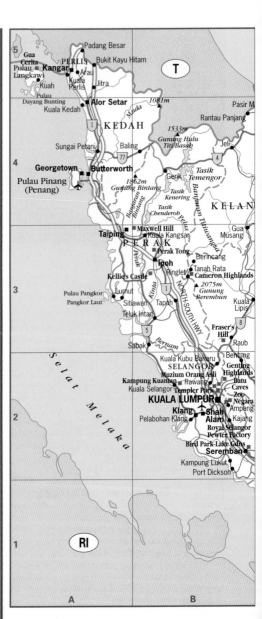

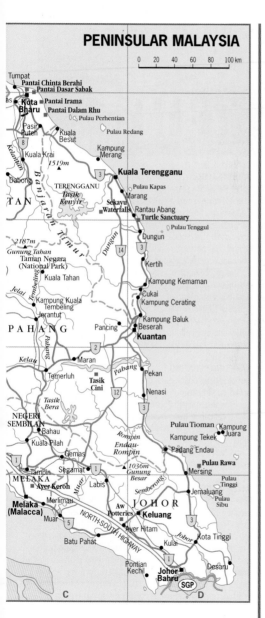

PENINSULAR MALAYSIA

0   20   40   60   80   100 km

Tumpat
Pantai Chinta Berahi
Pantai Dasar Sabak
Kota Bharu **Pantai Irama**
Pantai Dalam Rhu
Pulau Perhentian
Pasir Puteh
Kuala Besut
Pulau Redang
Kuala Krai
1519m
Kampung Merang
Dabong
TERENGGANU
Tasik Kenyir
Kuala Terengganu
Pulau Kapas
Marang
Sekayu Waterfalls
Rantau Abang
Turtle Sanctuary
Dungun
Pulau Tenggul
2187m
Gunung Tahan
Taman Negara (National Park)
Kertih
Kuala Tahan
Kampung Kemaman
Jelai
Cukai
Kampung Cerating
Kampung Kuala Tembeling
Jerantut
Kampung Baluk
Beserah
PAHANG
Pancing
Kuantan
Kelau
Maran
Temerluh
Tasik Cini
Pekan
Tasik Bera
Nenasi
NEGERI SEMBILAN
Bahau
Pulau Tioman Kampung Juara
Kuala Pilah
Rompin Endau-Rompin
Kampung Tekek
Padang Endau
Gemas
1036m
Gunung Besar
Pulau Rawa
Tampin
Segamat
Mersing
Pulau Tinggi
MELAKA
Ayer Keroh
Labis
Semberong
Jemaluang
Pulau Sibu
Melaka (Malacca)
Merlimau
Aw Potteries
JOHOR
Keluang
Muar
Ayer Hitam
Kota Tinggi
Batu Pahat
NORTH-SOUTH HIGHWAY
Kulai
Desaru
Pontian Kechil
Johor Bahru
SGP

C   D

Japanese Gardens in Ipoh (► 41)

43

 43D1
Muzium DiRaja Abu Bakar
✉ Jalan Air Molek
☎ (07) 223 0555
🕐 Daily 9–4
♿ None
💷 Expensive

Above: *the gleaming domes of Kuala Kangsar's Ubadiah Mosque*

 43D3
🍴 Bars; restaurants near by (£)

➕ 42B3
🗺 12km south of Ipoh, on A8 road between Gopeng and Batu Gajah
🕐 Daily 8:30–7:30
🍴 Café and picnic tables (£)
♿ None
💷 Cheap

JOHOR BAHRU ✪✪
Johor Bahru sits at the southern tip of the Malay peninsula, and is connected to the island of Singapore by a causeway. The city centre is currently undergoing extensive redevelopment, and shining new shopping malls and hotels rise above dilapidated shophouses and open drains. The development plan includes a pedestrianised city centre and landscaped waterfront.

The city is worth a visit just to see the **Muzium DiRaja Abu Bakar** (Royal Museum), a 19th-century palace set in beautifully landscaped grounds overlooking the Strait of Johor, a 10-minute walk from the centre. Built in 1866 for Sultan Abu Bakar, it is a treasure house of 19th-century Malay and European furniture, china, porcelain, crystal, and *objets d'art*, and evokes the wealth of the Malay sultans.

KAMPUNG CERATING ✪✪
Budget-priced beach-huts, chalets and restaurants line the broad curving bay of Cerating, a favourite backpackers' beach where makeshift bars serve cold beers in the shade of the casuarina trees overlooking the golden sands. The water is shallow and good for swimming at high water, but when the tide is out the bay is mostly dry. Asia's oldest Club Med is around the point to the north, next to Chendor Beach where turtles come ashore to lay their eggs.

KELLIE'S CASTLE ✪✪
This crumbling monument to the unrealised dreams of a wealthy British planter perches on a bluff above a small river. The four-storey Moorish mansion was begun in 1915 for William Kellie Smith, but remained unfinished following his death in 1926, and now stands in picturesque decrepitude. Near by is a small Hindu temple, complete with a figure of Smith on the roof, built to appease evil spirits after several labourers died of a mysterious disease. The building is in dangerous condition – do not enter it.

KOTA BHARU ✪✪✪

The state of Kelantan, in the far northeast of the peninsula, is often described as the cradle of Malay culture. Remote from the commercialised west and south, Malay customs and traditions have survived here undiluted. Kota Bharu, the state capital, has several interesting historic buildings, but its appeal lies more in its colourful markets and craft workshops. Padang Merdeka (Independence Square) lies next to the Kelantan River, surrounded by museums, notably the wooden palace of the Istana Jahar, built in 1887. More interesting, though, is the **Muzium Negeri** (State Museum), south of the centre.

Jalan Pejabat Pos Lama leads north from the Padang to the beach of Pantai Cinta Berahi, or 'PCB' (bus 10 from Central Market). The name means 'Beach of Passionate Love', which proved a little too *risqué* for the local authorities, who retained the acronym but renamed it Pantai Cahaya Bulan ('Moonlight Beach'). It is a pleasant strand of fine white sand, lined with palms and inexpensive motels, chalets and restaurants. The road to the beach is lined with Kelantan workshops selling batik, songket, kites, wood-carving, silverware and other crafts.

> 🔲 43C4
> **Muzium Negeri**
> ✉ Jalan Sultan Ibrahim
> 🕐 Sat–Thu 10:30–5.45.
> Closed Fri
> ✋ Cheap

Songket weaving in Kota Bharu

KOTA TINGGI ✪

The waterfalls at Kota Tinggi are a popular weekend picnic spot for local people, but during the week you can enjoy a swim in the deep, jungle-fringed pool below the upper fall in relative peace. The lower pools are safe for children.

> 🔲 43D1
> ✉ 9km from Lombong, signposted 'Air Terjun'
> 🕐 Daily 8AM–8PM
> 🍴 Restaurant and stalls (£)
> ✋ Cheap

KUALA KANGSAR ✪✪✪

Kuala Kangsar is a 'Royal Town' (Bandar Diraja), having been the seat of the sultans of Perak since the 18th century. It is famous for its magnificent Ubadiah Mosque, completed in 1917, whose huge, golden onion dome overlooks the river. Near by is the modern Royal Palace, and the **Muzium Istana Kenangan** (Royal Museum), housed in a wooden palace built in 1926 using neither plans nor nails. This served as temporary accommodation for the sultan while the new palace was built.

> 🔲 42B3
> **Muzium Istana Kenangan**
> ✉ Jalan Istana, Bukit Chandan
> ☎ (05) 776 5500
> 🕐 Sat–Wed 9:30–5, Thu 9:30–12.45. Closed Fri
> ♿ None
> ✋ Free

+ 42B2
Kampung Kuantan
✉ 10km east of Kuala Selangor
☎ (03) 889 2403 (reservations, 9–5)
🕓 Boat trips daily 8PM–11PM
💧 Moderate
❓ Package tours from KL available

+ 43C4
Muzium Negeri
✉ Bukit Losong, 3km south of city centre
☎ (09) 622 1444
🕓 Daily 10–6. Closed Fri 12–3
🍴 Café (£)
🚌 Losong minibus
♿ Few
💧 Moderate

Above: *the quiet waters of Kuala Selangor*

+ 43D3
🍴 Wide range (£–££)
🚌 39 from Kuantan to Teluk Cempedak

KUALA SELANGOR

This quiet backwater was once the seat of the Bugis sultans of Selangor, three of whom are buried on the wooded peak of Bukit Melawati, above the town. The summit of the hill is crowned by a lighthouse and the scant remains of 18th-century Fort Altinberg, overlooking the mouth of the Selangor River. On the coastal plain below are the mangrove forests of Taman Alam Kuala Selangor (► 68), a favourite haunt of local bird-watchers, while **Kampung Kuantan** (10km upstream) offers boat trips to see the spectacular evening displays of fireflies.

KUALA TERENGGANU

Money from offshore oil development has begun to change the face of the slightly down-at-heel capital of Terengganu state. Gleaming new office blocks now overlook the low-rise city centre, a modern luxury hotel has appeared behind the beach at Pantai Batu Buruk, and a few of the crumbling Chinese shophouses along Jalan Bandar have been restored as craft and souvenir shops. The city is largely neglected by tourists, but it is worth at least half a day. The main attractions in the city centre are the lively and colourful Central Market and the traditional boat-building yards on Pulau Duyung.

Kuala Terengganu's biggest draw, however, is the magnificent new **Muzium Negeri** (State Museum) complex. Three vast, interconnected halls, echoing the style of traditional wooden architecture, house one of Malaysia's best-presented museums, with exhibits covering history, nature, decorative arts, weaponry, ceramics, archaeology and Islam. The separate Petroleum Gallery explains where the money for this impressive complex came from. The grounds contain further exhibits, including a Maritime Museum with two traditional wooden *putera* trading vessels.

KUANTAN

The state capital of Pahang is a pleasant city at the mouth of the Kuantan River. Apart from the colourful waterfront along Jalan Besar, there is little to see or do except head

4km out of town to the beach at Teluk Cempedak, a golden strand with several luxury hotels, a lively promenade and plenty of watersports facilities.

MARANG ✪✪

Not to be confused with Kampung Merang to the north, Marang is a picturesque fishing village 15km south of Kuala Terengganu. A narrow lagoon, packed with colourful fishing boats and spanned by two footbridges, separates the mainland village from the stilted wooden houses of the fishermen's *kampung* on a palm-fringed sand-spit beside the river mouth. Marang has been a popular hang-out for backpackers for many years, but now medium-range hotels are being added to the beach-huts and chalets. The village is also the point of departure for Pulau Kapas (► 55), clearly visible offshore.

🚹 43C4

🍴 Guest-house restaurants overlooking lagoon (£); restaurants at resort hotels (££)

🚢 Boats to Pulau Kapas can be arranged at guest-houses/resort hotels

Maxwell Hill

MAXWELL HILL (BUKIT LARUT) ✪✪✪

Maxwell Hill is the oldest, smallest and least developed of Malaysia's hill resorts. It is also the wettest place in the country, receiving a drenching 5,000mm of rain each year. The narrow, winding road to the 1,100m summit is closed to private vehicles, and access is by a government-run Land Rover shuttle service. Limited accommodation is available in a handful of rustic wooden bungalows, and activities rarely stretch beyond strolling in the gardens and enjoying the views from your veranda.

🚹 42B3

✉ 12km northeast of Taiping

☎ Enquiries and reservations: (05) 807 7241

🍴 Meals available at Maxwell Rest House (£)

🚌 Land Rover shuttle runs hourly, 8–6

♿ None

47

Melaka

The name Melaka (formerly spelt 'Malacca') conjures up romantic images of the Orient: sailing ships at anchor in the strait, cargoes of tea, opium and silk, palm-fringed harbours and the exotic scents of sandalwood and spice. Though long since overtaken by the 20th century, the ancient trading port of Melaka manages to preserve more history than any other Malaysian town.

A worshipper lights a candle at Cheng Hoon Teng Chinese temple

Founded by a Sumatran prince in the early 15th century, and held at various times by the Portuguese, the Dutch and the British, Melaka has had a long and turbulent history. The old town is clustered around the mouth of the Melaka River, and all the main sights are within easy walking distance. Many of the oldest buildings, such as the Stadthuys, St Paul's Church and the fortress gate of A Famosa, are found on and around Bukit St Paul (St Paul's Hill), whose summit offers a fine view over the town. Across the river is Chinatown, a grid of streets lined with shophouses and Peranakan mansions centred on Jonkers Street, a hunting ground for antiques and souvenirs.

Melaka's pot-pourri of cultures is most evident in its cuisine, which betrays influences from Indonesia, China, India, Arabia, and Portugal. The town is best-known for Nyonya cuisine, served in a number of restaurants set in old Melaka town-houses. Other delights can be sampled among the hawkers' stalls at Gluttons' Corner (➤ 95).

What to See in the City Centre

A FAMOSA

When the Portuguese captured Melaka in 1511 they built this fortress to defend their settlement on St Paul's Hill. The Dutch rebuilt the fortifications in 1670, but in 1808 the British ordered its destruction. Sir Thomas Stamford Raffles, then a government agent in Pinang, intervened, to preserve the Porta de Santiago gate, which still stands. The stucco relief above the arch commemorates the Dutch renovation (the soldier on the right bears the arms of the Dutch East India Company, 'VOC', on his shield).

BABA-NYONYA HERITAGE MUSEUM

This privately owned museum is a monument to the unique Peranakan ('intermarriage') culture of Melaka. The Babas and Nyonyas ('gentlemen' and 'ladies') are descended from Chinese immigrants who intermarried with local Malays and adopted many of their traditions. This Peranakan mansion was built in 1896 and is furnished in period style.

CHENG HOON TENG

Malaysia's oldest Chinese temple, dating from 1646 and dedicated to Kuan Yin (goddess of mercy), was built using materials and craftsmen shipped from China. Colourful ceramic sculpture, gilded wood-carving and lacquerwork surround the three altars, which represent the paths of Buddhism, Taoism and Confucianism.

CHRIST CHURCH

The bright red façade of Christ Church dominates Dutch Square in the heart of old Melaka. Built by the Dutch in 1753, it retains its original hand-carved wooden pews, and massive roof-beams, each hewn from a single tree-trunk. On the floor are old tombs carved in Dutch and Armenian; more Dutch and British gravestones can be found in the Dutch graveyard at the foot of St Paul's Hill.

43C1
Jalan Kota
Muzium Budaya, St Paul's Church (➤ 51)

Above: a detail of the remarkable carving that decorates Cheng Hoon Teng's exterior

43C1
Jalan Tun Tan Cheng Lock
(06) 283 1273
Daily 10–12:30, 2–4:30. Guided tour only, duration 45 mins
None Moderate

43C1
Jalan Tokong
Early till late (no fixed hours)
Masjid Kampung Kling (➤ 50)

43C1
Dutch Square
Daily
Stadthuys (➤ 51)

43C1
✉ Jalan Laksamana
☎ None
🕐 Daily 9–6 (9PM Sat–Sun).
   Closed Fri 12:15–2:45
🍴 Drinks stall (£)
♿ None
💵 Cheap

MARITIME MUSEUM

Housed in a re-creation of a Portuguese ship, this museum tells the story of Melaka's maritime history, illustrated with ship models, old nautical charts and objects recovered from shipwrecks. The 'deck' provides a good view along the Melaka River. The ticket includes admission to the Royal Malaysian Navy Museum across the road, which has a display of relics recovered from the *Diana*, which sank off Melaka in 1817 with a cargo of china, tea and sugar, while on passage from Guangzhou to Madras.

43C1
✉ Jalan Kampung Hulu
🕐 Closed to non-Muslims

MASJID KAMPUNG HULU

Built in 1728, this is the oldest surviving mosque in Malaysia. The unusual architectural style shows Sumatran influence, with a triple-tiered pyramidal roof clad in green ceramic tiles, and an octagonal minaret rather like a lighthouse. Most of Melaka's mosques are modelled on Kampung Hulu.

43C1
✉ Jalan Tokong Emas
🕐 Daily, except at prayer
   times

MASJID KAMPUNG KLING

This mosque, set in the heart of Chinatown, dates from 1748. Its eclectic style shares the Sumatran influence of Masjid Kampung Hulu, but the square, tapered minaret resembles a Moorish tower, the prayer hall contains Corinthian columns and a British Victorian chandelier, and the walls are decorated with English and Portuguese ceramic tiles.

43C1
✉ Jalan Parameswara
🕐 Tue–Sun 9–6. Closed
   Mon; Fri 12–3
🍴 Drinks stalls nearby
💵 Free
↔ Muzium Budaya
   (► below)

MEMORIAL PERGISTIHARAN KEMERDEKAAN (INDEPENDENCE MEMORIAL HALL)

Once the premises of the Malacca Club, this 1912 villa is Melaka's only surviving British colonial building. It was here that Tuanku Abdul Rahman, the first prime minister of Malaya, announced independence in 1957. The villa is now a museum tracing the struggle for independence. Tuanku Abdul Rahman's blue '57 Chevrolet is on display outside.

Left: *a royal audience re-created in the Muzium Budaya (Cultural Museum)*

MUZIUM BUDAYA (CULTURAL MUSEUM) ✪✪✪

A description in the *Sejarah Melayu* (the 17th-century *Malay Annals*,) formed the basis for this magnificent wooden reconstruction of the 15th-century royal palace of the Sultan of Melaka, put together using traditional dove-tailing techniques. Not a single metal nail was needed. The palace houses exhibits depicting the sultan's court and other aspects of Malay culture, including costumes, weapons, musical instruments and traditional games.

✚	43C1
✉	Jalan Kota
☎	(06) 282 0769
🕐	Daily 9–6. Closed Fri 12:15–2:45
🍴	Drinks stalls near by (£)
♿	None
🎟	Cheap
↔	A Famosa (➤ 49)

ST PAUL'S CHURCH ✪✪✪

The ruins of this little church enjoy a lovely hilltop setting, shaded by tall trees and looking out over the river to the sea. The church was built in 1521 by the Portuguese who called it Our Lady of the Hill; it was renamed St Paul's by the Dutch, who abandoned it following the completion of their own Christ Church. St Francis Xavier preached here in 1545, and his remains were briefly interred here following his death in 1553, before being removed to Goa in India; a marble statue of the saint stands outside.

✚	43C1
✉	St Paul's Hill
↔	A Famosa (➤ 49)

Below: *cyclists parking outside the sturdy Stadthuys (Town Hall)*

STADTHUYS ✪✪✪

The Stadthuys (Town Hall), built in the 1650s to house the Dutch governors of Melaka and their administrative offices, is a fine example of 17th-century Dutch colonial archi-tecture, with stout masonry walls and heavy timber doors, and polished wooden floors and louvered windows on the upper storeys. Displays cover the history of Melaka from its foundation in 1400 to the 20th century.

✚	43C1
✉	Dutch Square
🕐	Daily 9–6. Closed Fri 12:15–2:45
🍴	Cold drinks vending machine (£)
🎟	Cheap
↔	Christ Church (➤ 49)

51

A Walk Around Melaka

Distance
3km

Time
1 hour, excluding time spent visiting attractions

Start point
Tourist Information Office, Dutch Square
✚ 43C1

End point
A Famosa (➤ 49)
✚ 43C1

Lunch
Heeren House Café (££)
✉ 1 Jalan Tun Tan Cheng Lock
☎ (06) 281 4241

On this walk you can enjoy striking architecture, historical sites and the hubbub of Melaka's busy centre.

Turn left from the tourist office and cross the bridge over the Melaka River into Chinatown. Turn left again at the OCBC Bank along Lorong Hang Jebat, then right at the Heeren House Hotel into Jalan Tun Tan Cheng Lock.

This street is lined with traditional Peranakan mansions, with colourful tiles, carved wooden doors and shutters decorated with gold Chinese characters. Halfway along on the right is the ornate tiled façade of the Baba-Nyonya Heritage Museum (➤ 49).

Continue past Jalan Hang Lekir, and turn right at Jalan Kubu.

Here the main road leads to the tiny Tamil Methodist Church, built in 1908.

Turn right in front of the church into Jalan Tokong, and bear left where the road forks.

A narrow street crammed with vegetable stalls leads past the Cheng Hoon Teng Temple (➤ 49) on the right.

Turn right along an alley (Jalan Lekiu) in front of the Masjid Kampung Kling to reach Jalan Hang Jebat (formerly Jonkers Street, famed for its antique shops). Go left to reach the bridge and cross back to Dutch Square. Go up the covered stairs past the Stadthuys (➤ 51), past the old fire engine, and up the stairs across the road. Go right along the path at the top to reach St Paul's Church (➤ 51). Follow the path to the right of the church and descend to A Famosa (➤ 49) and the Muzium Budaya (➤ 51).

A screen inlaid with mother-of-pearl, displayed at the Baba-Nyonya Heritage Museum

MERLIMAU ✪

The road from Melaka south to Muar passes many fine examples of lovely old Melakan houses, in which Chinese motifs are blended with the traditional Malay style of architecture. These wooden houses are raised on stilts (for ventilation, and to deter snakes and rodents), and have an open veranda at the front, a living area in the middle, and a kitchen at the back. The Chinese influence is seen in the colourful front staircase, decorated with ceramic tiles, and the intricate wood carving that embellishes the eaves. Penghulu's House, 2km south of the village of Merlimau, is a fine example of the style. It was built in 1894 for the village chief, and still belongs to his descendants.

✚ 43C1
✉ 25km south of Melaka
🚌 2 from Melaka to Muar

Above: *a village hut in the Muzium Orang Asli*

MERSING ✪

The bustling fishing port of Mersing is the jumping-off point for exploring the archipelago of coral-fringed islands that lies scattered offshore. The most popular is the beautiful resort island of Pulau Tioman (➤ 25), but there are many others, including tiny Pulau Rawa (➤ 65), the 600m extinct volcano of Pulau Tinggi and the remote and idyllic retreats of Pulau Pemanggil and Pulau Aur.

✚ 43D2
Mersing Tourist Information Office
✉ Jalan Abu Bakar
☎ (07) 799 5212
🕐 Daily 8–12:45, 2–4:20. Closed Fri PM

MUZIUM ORANG ASLI ✪✪

The term *Orang Asli* (literally 'original people') refers to the aboriginal tribes who have inhabited Peninsular Malaysia since prehistoric times. A population of about 60,000 Orang Asli survive today, most of them living in primitive villages in the forest. This small museum lies on the road to Genting Highlands, and its collection of farming tools, blow-pipes, animal traps, weapons, basketry, musical instruments and carved idols provides a fascinating insight into Orang Asli culture.

✚ 42B2
✉ Gombak
☎ (03) 689 2122
🕐 Sun–Thu 9–5. Closed Fri
✋ Free

🞣 43C4
🚌 Bus 3 from Kota Bharu to Pasir Puteh, then 96 to Kuala Besut

PANTAI DALAM RHU ✪✪

Sometimes known as Pantai Bisikan Bayu (Beach of the Whispering Breeze), this is the prettiest of Kelantan's beaches, a long stretch of alabaster sand overhung by the feathery limbs of casuarina trees. It lies near the fishing village of Semerak (about 50km south of Kota Bharu), and is a 10-minute walk from the road.

🞣 43C5
🚌 8 or 9 from Kota Bharu to Sabak

PANTAI DASAR SABAK ✪

On 7 December 1941, more than an hour before the first bombs fell on Pearl Harbour, the Japanese entered World War II when they began their invasion of the Malay peninsula by landing on this peaceful, palm-fringed beach. Today, all that remains is a crumbling concrete bunker. Colourful local fishing boats haul out on the beach at nearby Kampung Sabak to unload and sell their catch.

🞣 43C4
🍴 Refreshment stalls (£)
🚌 Bus 2a, 2b from Kota Bharu to Bacok

PANTAI IRAMA ✪

Pantai Irama (Melody Beach) is near the village of Bacok, about 25km southeast of Kota Bharu. A narrow lagoon, spanned by foot-bridges, separates the sand-spit beach from a landscaped promenade with a few food and drinks stalls.

🞣 43D2
Muzium Sultan Abu Bakar
✉ Jalan Sultan Ahmad
🕐 Tue–Sun 9:30–5 (Fri 9–12:15). Closed Mon
♿ None
👝 Cheap

PEKAN ✪✪

This pleasantly sleepy town on the south bank of the broad Pahang River is a royal town (Bandar DiRaja), the seat of the sultans of Pahang. The modern royal palace (Istana Abu Bakar) lies about a kilometre back from the river, surrounded by the immaculate turf of the Royal Golf Club and the Royal Polo Club, but it is not open to the public. Head instead for the waterfront, where the old British Residency houses the **Muzium Sultan Abu Bakar**

Messing about on the water off the lovely shores of Pulau Kapas

(State Museum), easily recognised by the jet-fighter parked in the gardens. Exhibits include royal costumes and jewellery, traditional weapons, Chinese ceramics and natural history. There is a small zoo in the grounds, and a white-tiled pavilion on a little island opposite the museum contains a display of traditional boat-building. The road south from Pekan towards Mersing follows the largely uninhabited coast, past miles of deserted, sandy beach.

PORT DICKSON ✪

Port Dickson, popularly known as 'PD', was a thriving 19th-century harbour used for the export of tin ore. Today it is the gateway to the 17km of beach that stretch south to the lighthouse of Cape Rachado, overrun at weekends by city-dwellers from Seremban and KL. The beaches are far from idyllic, as the water is shallow and murky and the view is often spoiled by oil tankers anchored in the strait, but the coast is lined with dozens of resort hotels, all of which have good swimming pools, where you can rent boats to take you to more peaceful beaches on the offshore islands.

🚹 42B2

PULAU KAPAS ✪✪✪

A 30-minute boat trip from Marang (➤ 47) takes you to the beautiful little island of Kapas, with its picture-postcard white-sand beaches and sparkling turquoise waters. It is a popular day-trip destination so if you want peace and quiet, avoid weekends and public holidays. The most popular beaches are on the west coast, but trails lead along the shore and across the island to quieter coves. There is excellent snorkelling around the nearby islet of Pulau Raja. Accommodation is available in several low-key chalet developments.

🚹 43D4
🛥 Boat trips can be arranged in Marang

PULAU LANGKAWI (► 22–3, TOP TEN)

PULAU PANGKOR ✪✪✪

The island of Pangkor, only 10km long and 4km wide, is renowned for its golden beaches, and is a popular weekend retreat for local city-dwellers, but on weekdays the beaches are deserted. Pangkor Town, on the east side of the island, is a lively strip of market stalls, shops, temples, jetties, boat-yards and fish-drying racks, from which a single road leads around the coast to the outlying beaches and fishing villages. The best beaches, with white sands backed by rounded granite outcrops and jungle, are in the north and west, notably at Teluk Nipah, Coral Bay and Teluk Belanga. The island's only historical attraction is the 17th-century Dutch fort of Kota Belanda, in the southeast.

PULAU PERHENTIAN ✪✪✪

These two islands – Pulau Perhentian Besar (Big Island) and Pulau Perhentian Kecil (Little Island) – lie 21km off the east coast, and are often described as the most beautiful islands in Malaysia. Each is less than 5km across, covered in thick jungle, and surrounded by coral reefs and beaches of pristine white sand. Like Pulau Redang (► 65) they lie within the Terengganu Marine Park, and are popular with scuba divers and snorkellers (the diving season is May to October, when the waters are at their clearest). The only village is on Pulau Kecil, but most of the accommodation, in the form of a single resort development and a range of budget chalets, is on Pulau Besar.

✚ 42A3
🚢 30-minute ferry crossing from Lumut, 90km southwest of Ipoh

---

✚ 43C4
🍴 Several beach restaurants (£–££)
🚢 Boat trips can be arranged at Kuala Besut on the mainland; the crossing to the islands takes about two hours

The beauty of Pulau Perhentian Besar and Pulau Perhentian Kecil attracts many visitors

Pulau Pinang (Penang)

Pulau Pinang, or 'Betel Nut Island', is one of Malaysia's favourite tourist destinations. Its varied attractions include the palm-fringed beaches of Batu Feringgi and Teluk Bahang; the panoramic views of Pinang Hill; traditional *kampungs*; and the lively city of Georgetown, with its historic colonial buildings, colourful temples and fascinating Chinatown streets.

Enjoy the cool breezes and magnificent views from Pinang Hill

Pulau Pinang's strategic location at the northern entrance to the Strait of Malacca led Captain Francis Light to acquire the island as a naval base for the British East India Company in 1786. He built Fort Cornwallis to protect the harbour, and founded the settlement of Georgetown, named after King George III.

The island measures roughly 25km north to south by 15km east to west, and is linked to the mainland by the 13.5km-long Pinang Bridge. Georgetown, in the northeast, is an attractive city of half a million people, with a thriving Chinese community (► 24). The north coast has several good, sandy beaches, though the sea around the island is rather murky compared with the crystal waters of Tioman and Langkawi. The coastal plains of the west and south are largely given over to *padi* fields, while the east coast is heavily industrialised along the highway between Georgetown and the international airport at Bayan Lepas. Bukit Bendera (821m), the highest point on the island, has its own miniature hill resort, complete with a tea kiosk, a hotel and a funicular railway.

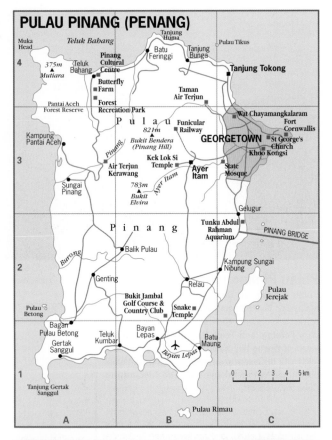

PULAU PINANG (PENANG)

4

Muka Head

Teluk Bahang

Tanjung Huma

Batu Feringgi

Tanjung Bunga

Pulau Tikus

375m ▲ *Mutiara*

Teluk Bahang

Pinang Cultural Centre

Tanjung Tokong

Butterfly Farm

Taman Air Terjun

Pantai Aceh Forest Reserve

Forest Recreation Park

P u l a u

Funicular Railway

Wat Chayamangkalaram

Fort Cornwallis

3

Kampung Pantai Aceh

821m ▲ *Bukit Bendera (Pinang Hill)*

GEORGETOWN

St George's Church

Air Terjun Kerawang

Kek Lok Si Temple

Ayer Itam

State Mosque

Khoo Kongsi

Sungai Pinang

Pinang

783m ▲ *Bukit Elvira*

Ayer Itam

Gelugur

P i n a n g

Tunku Abdul Rahman Aquarium

PINANG BRIDGE

2

Burong

Balik Pulau

Kampung Sungai Nibung

Genting

Relau

Pulau Jerejak

Bukit Jambal Golf Course & Country Club

Snake Temple

Pulau Betong

Bagan Pulau Betong

Teluk Kumbar

Bayan Lepas

Batu Maung

Gertak Sanggul

Bayan Lepas

1

Tanjung Gertak Sanggul

0 1 2 3 4 5 km

Pulau Rimau

A   **B**   **C**

What to See in Georgetown

CHINATOWN ✪✪✪

Georgetown's Chinatown is the biggest and best preserved in Malaysia. Centred on Lebuh Chulia, its maze of streets is jammed with people, cars and bicycle rickshaws, and lined with pre-war shophouses, temples and workshops. You could spend half a day wandering among the back streets, discovering antique shops, rattan furniture makers, goldsmiths, Chinese coffin workshops, birdcage sellers and clan houses, assaulted by the everyday sounds and smells of Chinatown – the rattle of moped engines and the clatter of *mah-jongg* tiles, the sweet fragrance of joss-sticks and jasmine blossom mingling with the aroma of stir-fried meat and the occasional whiff of open drains.

☩ 60B1
✉ Lebuh Pantai to Jalan Pinang

Browsing in Georgetown, the best city for shopping

FORT CORNWALLIS ✪✪

The crumbling bastions of Fort Cornwallis, which replaced the original timber palisade at the beginning of the 19th century, mark the site of the earliest British settlement on Pinang Island. Little remains of the fort apart from the ramparts, which are surmounted by a number of ancient cannons. The biggest, known as Seri Ramabai, was cast in 1603 and given by the Dutch to the Sultan of Johor. Behind the cannon is the old powder magazine, which houses a small exhibition on the fort's history. Cultural shows are regularly performed in the auditorium in the middle of the fort.

The ornate clock tower to the south of the fort was presented to the town by a local millionaire to mark the Diamond Jubilee of Queen Victoria in 1897.

☩ 60C2
✉ Lebuh Light
🕐 Daily 8:30–7
🍴 Drinks stall (£)
♿ None
🎫 Cheap

Opposite page: *ancestors of the Khoo family are honoured in the magnificent Khoo Kongsi*

KHOO KONGSI (CLAN HOUSE) ✪✪✪

Members of the Khoo family sponsored the construction of this magnificent clan house at the end of the 19th century, as a combined meeting hall and temple for the worship of their ancestors. The hall is beautifully decorated with elaborate wood-carvings of Chinese mythical scenes, colourful ceramic tiles and sculptures, and ornate wrought-iron work. The dark-wood interior conceals altars shrouded in incense smoke and gilded tablets commemorating the Khoo ancestors.

☩ 60B1
✉ Cannon Square, off Lebuh Cannon
🕐 Mon–Fri 9–5, Sat 9–1. Closed Sun
♿ None
🎫 Free, but ask permission to enter from office in alley leading from Lebuh Cannon

59

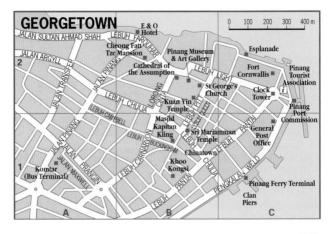

GEORGETOWN

KUAN YIN TENG (KUAN YIN TEMPLE)

Pinang's oldest Chinese temple, dating from 1800, is dedicated to the goddess of mercy, Kuan Yin, and guarded by two blue ceramic dragons snaking along the ornately decorated roof. Braziers burn in the courtyard, and worshippers bearing offerings of joss-sticks, paper money and flowers bow before the altars. This is one of the more modest examples of temple architecture in Georgetown.

MASJID KAPITAN KLING
(KAPITAN KLING MOSQUE)

This mosque, with its distinctive yellow domes and Moorish minaret, was founded at the end of the 18th century by the 'Kapitan Kling', the head-man of the South Indian Tamil (*Keling* in Malay) community. The Tamils (Indian Muslims)

Worshippers offer joss-sticks at Kuan Yin Teng

60

came to Pinang as sepoys under the command of Captain Francis Light. The mosque was rebuilt in 1916, and visitors are welcome provided they are suitably dressed (▶ 70–1).

PINANG MUSEUM AND ART GALLERY ✪✪

A statue of Captain Francis Light, the founder of Georgetown, stands in front of the elegant museum building, which dates from 1821. The exhibits chart Pinang's colourful history with old photographs, documents, paintings and engravings, and displays of furniture, costumes, weapons, porcelain and other items salvaged from both the colonial and Chinese communities, including a Chinese bridal chamber and early trishaws. One of the original wooden cars from the Pinang Hill funicular railway (see Bukit Bendera, ▶ 62) can be seen in the garden.

ST GEORGE'S CHURCH ✪

The slender white spire and classical portico of St George's Church date from 1818. Built using convict labour, it is the oldest Anglican church in Southeast Asia, and sits in a grassy park shaded by the original *angsana* trees that were planted at the time of its construction. The circular pavilion in front of the church is a memorial to Captain Light, who died of malaria in 1794.

WAT CHAYAMANGKALARAM ✪✪

This brightly painted Thai Buddhist temple houses a 33m-long gilded figure of the reclining Buddha, one of the biggest of its kind in existence. The image is guarded by colourful statues of serpents and warriors in the courtyard outside. (Note that no photography is allowed inside the temple.) An equally interesting Burmese temple lies just across the road.

The giant reclining Buddha at Wat Chayamangkalaram

✚ 60B2
✉ Lebuh Farquhar
☎ (04) 261 3144
🕐 Daily 9–5. Closed Fri 12:15–2:45
♿ None
🎟 Free
↔ St George's Church (▶ below)

✚ 60B2
✉ Lebuh Farquhar
🕐 Daily
♿ None
↔ Pinang Museum and Art Gallery (▶ above)

✚ 58C3
✉ Lorong Burma, off Jalan Kelawai
🕐 Early morning–late evening
🚌 Buses 2, 93, 94, 95
♿ None
🎟 Free

What to See Around Pulau Pinang

BATU FERINGGI ✪✪

Batu Feringgi (Foreigner's Rock) is Pinang's biggest and most famous beach resort. The 3km strand of golden sand is backed by shady casuarina trees and a string of luxury hotels, and the main road is lined with restaurants, bars, batik shops, money-changers and car and motorbike rentals. The beach is beautifully clean and well-groomed, but the sea is murky and suffers from pollution; all the hotels have good swimming pools. In the evening the main strip comes alive with market stalls and hawkers.

BUKIT BENDERA (PINANG HILL) ✪✪✪

Bukit Bendera (Flag Hill), now more commonly called Pinang Hill, is the oldest of Malaysia's hill resorts. Its 821m summit was cleared for strawberry-growing soon after the settlement of Georgetown, and quickly became a popular retreat for wealthy colonials, as the climate is on average 5°C cooler than that on the coast. Access was by pack-horse or sedan chair until the construction of a Swiss-designed funicular railway in 1923. The funicular journey takes 30 minutes, including a change of trains at the halfway point; the original wooden carriages, which were recently replaced with modern ones, can be seen in the museums at Georgetown and Kuala Lumpur. Today the summit has a hotel, a mosque, a Hindu temple and a network of walking trails, including the original road which descends to Jalan Air Terjun near the entrance to the Botanical Gardens (see Taman Air Terjun, below). The views are especially good around sunset, but the last train down can be very crowded.

BUTTERFLY FARM ✪✪

This landscaped park with water-falls, rock garden, lily pond and bubbling mud pool contains thousands of free-flying butterflies, plus displays of other tropical insects such as scorpions, spiders, stick and leaf insects, and giant millipedes.

✚ 58B4
✉ 14km northwest of Georgetown
🍴 Restaurants and bars (£–£££)
🚌 Bus 93
♿ Few

✚ 58B3
✉ Ayer Itam, 6km west of Georgetown
☎ Pinang Tourist Information Office: (04) 261 9067
🕐 Trains run daily every 30 mins, 6:30AM–9:30PM
🍴 Restaurant, tea kiosk, hawker centre (£–££)
🚌 Bus 1 or 91, minibus 21to Ayer Itam, then bus 8
♿ None
💲 Cheap
↔ Kek Lok Si Temple, Taman Air Terjun (► below)

✚ 58A4
✉ Teluk Bahang
☎ (04) 885 1253
🕐 Daily 9–5 (6PM weekends and hols)
🍴 Cold drinks (£)
🚌 Bus 93 from Georgetown
♿ None
💲 Cheap
↔ Teluk Bahang (► below)

The golden spire of the Pagoda of Ten Thousand Buddhas, in the Kek Lok Si temple complex

KEK LOK SI TEMPLE ✪✪✪

This huge temple complex was begun in 1890, and is still being expanded today. The central feature is the 30m-tall Pagoda of Ten Thousand Buddhas with its golden, Burmese-style spire, overlooked by a huge, hilltop statue of Kuan Yin, the goddess of mercy. The complex includes several courtyards, shrines and pavilions, and a crowded craft and souvenir bazaar.

➕ 58B3
✉ Ayer Itam, 6km west of Georgetown
🕓 Daily, early till late
🚌 Bus 1 or 91, minibus 21
♿ None
💷 Free; donation to climb pagoda
↔ Bukit Bendera (▶ above)

TAMAN AIR TERJUN (BOTANICAL GARDENS) ✪✪

Laid out by the British in 1884, these 30-hectare gardens incorporate a scenic waterfall and a number of tranquil jungle walks, but their main feature is the troops of leaf monkeys who boldly pester anyone who appears to be in possession of edible items – picnickers beware! A hiking trail leads to the summit of Bukit Bendera (▶ above); the climb takes about three hours.

➕ 58B4
✉ Jalan Kebun Bunga, 8km northwest of Georgetown
🕓 Daily 5AM–8PM
🍴 Café stalls (£–££)
🚌 Bus 7
♿ Few
💷 Free
↔ Bukit Bendera (▶ above)

TELUK BAHANG ✪✪

Resort developments are gradually encroaching upon this fishing village, which marks the end of the north-coast beach strip. Fishing boats land their catches at the long jetty at the west end of the beach, and the village restaurants are famed for their fresh fish and juicy prawns. Hiking trails lead west along the coast as far as the light-house on Muka Head, passing some beautiful beaches (which can also be reached by boat from Teluk Bahang and Batu Feringgi).

➕ 58A4
✉ 20km northwest of Georgetown
🍴 Village restaurants (£–££)
🚌 Bus 93
♿ None
↔ Butterfly Farm (▶ above)
❓ Cultural shows at Pinang Cultural Centre, daily at 10:15, noon and 3:15

63

A Tour of Pinang Island

Distance
70km

Time
2 hours, not including time
spent at attractions

Start/end point
Georgetown
⊞ 58C3

Lunch
End of the World Restaurant
(£)
✉ Jalan Hassan Abas, Teluk
Bahang
☎ (04) 881 1189

*Inhabitant at the Penang
Butterfly Farm*

This drive makes an anti-clockwise circuit of the island. Try to get back to Georgetown before the evening rush hour, which begins around 4:30PM.

Leave Georgetown on Jalan Sultan Ahmad Shah.

The route passes the Penang Club and numerous luxurious villas; during colonial times this was called Northam Road, and was home to the city's wealthy merchants.

Follow signs for Tanjung Tokong and Batu Feringgi.

The road winds through the beach-front developments of Tanjung Tokong and Tanjung Bunga, but the best beaches are beyond the resort of Batu Feringgi (➤ 62).

Another 5km of twisting coastal road leads to Teluk Bahang (➤ 63). At the roundabout in the middle of the village go straight on to reach the End of the World Restaurant; otherwise turn left.

The road passes a batik factory, then the Penang Butterfly Farm (➤ 62), before climbing steeply into the jungle-clad hills. As it begins to descend on the far side, it passes the Air Terjun Kerawang (Kerawang Waterfall), where fruit stalls line the verge. You can stop here and walk a short distance up a path to admire the falls, festooned with luxuriant vegetation.

The road descends to the plain and passes through a series of Malay kampungs with traditional wooden stilt houses. Follow signs for Balik Pulau, and then for Bayan Lepas, passing through the fishing village of Teluk Kumbar at the southern end of the island. There is nothing worth seeing on the industrialised east coast, so simply follow the highway from Bayan Lepas back to Georgetown.

PULAU RAWA ✪✪

The tiny island of Rawa lies 16km from the coast at Mersing (► 53). It offers fine, coral-sand beaches, good fishing, and reasonable snorkelling and diving, though much of the coral around the island is now dead (arrange a boat trip to one of the neighbouring islands for better coral reefs). There is only one place to stay on the island, and it is in great demand at weekends, so book ahead and try to visit mid-week.

➕ 43D2
Rawa Safaris Island Resort
✉ Jalan Abu Bakar, Mersing (Booking Office)
☎ (07) 799 1204
🍽 Restaurant and bar (£–££)
🚤 Resort boat service

PULAU REDANG ✪✪✪

For many years Pulau Redang was a secret known only to scuba divers, the three- to four-hour boat journey from Kampung Merang deterring all but the most adventurous travellers. Nowadays, a 150-room luxury beach resort, complete with 9-hole golf course, has joined the island's camping grounds and chalet developments, and high-speed boats can make the crossing in little more than an hour. Pulau Redang lies 45km from the coast, well out of reach of pollution and river silt, and its surrounding coral reefs support a remarkable diversity of marine life, including turtles, reef sharks, sea-horses, stingrays and a multitude of brilliantly coloured tropical fish. Redang and eight other islands are protected within the Terengganu Marine Park, where fishing and coral collecting are banned, and diving, snorkelling and water sports are controlled. Apart from diving, the main attractions are the island beaches of white coral sand, and the breathtaking sunsets. Strong winds and rough seas can make the island inaccessible during the east coast monsoon (November to March).

➕ 43C4
🍽 Restaurants in resort hotels and campgrounds (£–£££)
🚤 No regular ferry service; boats must be hired at Kampung Merang

Colourful fish

Right and below: *turtles struggle up the east coast beaches of Peninsular Malaysia to lay their eggs*

PULAU TIOMAN (➤ 25, TOP TEN)

RANTAU ABANG ✪✪✪
TURTLE SANCTUARY

Peninsular Malaysia's east coast, from Kampung Cerating (➤ 44) north to Rantau Abang, is one of only six known sites in the world where the leatherback turtle (*Dermochelys coriacea*) comes ashore to lay its eggs. These majestic creatures, which can attain a length of over 2m and a weight of 550kg, roam the seas for most of the year (turtles tagged on Malaysian beaches have been found in the Atlantic Ocean), but between June and September the females come ashore to lay their eggs in the sand. The peak season is August, when the turtles lumber up the beaches under cover of darkness, and excavate a hole in the sand before laying a clutch of 50 to 150 eggs. The eggs take about eight weeks to hatch, and the tiny hatchlings must make a perilous journey down the beach to the safety of the sea. The coast for 10km on either side of Rantau Abang has been designated a turtle sanctuary, but certain areas have been set aside for viewing the nesting turtles. The **Turtle Information Centre** has exhibits and film shows on the turtles' natural history, and provides details of turtle-watching trips.

 43D4
Turtle Information Centre
✉ 13th Mile Jalan Dungun
☎ (09) 844 1533
🕐 May–Aug, Sat–Thu 9–1, 2–6, 8–11, Fri 9–noon, 3–11; Sep–Apr, Sat–Wed 8–12:45, 2–4, Thu 8–12:45. Closed Fri and public hols
🚌 Regular buses from Kuala Terengganu and Dungun
🚐 Guided turtle-watching trips: cheap

ROYAL SELANGOR PEWTER FACTORY ✪

The world's largest manufacturer of pewterware was founded in 1885 by a Chinese immigrant to Malaya called Yong Koon, and the family company is still owned by his descendants. The guided tour of the factory allows you to watch craftsmen at work before browsing in the adjoining showroom, outside which stands the world's largest beer tankard – it weighs 1,557kg and can hold 2,790 litres.

🔲 42B2
✉ 4 Jalan Usahawan Enam, Setapak Jaya, Selangor
☎ (03) 422 1000
🕐 Mon–Sat 8:30–4:45, Sun, public hols 9–4
🚌 Bus 167, 169 from KL
🚐 Free

SEREMBAN ✪✪

Seremban is the capital of Negeri Sembilan, a small west-coast state with an unusual cultural legacy. Immigrants from the Minangkabau culture of Sumatra settled in the area, and in the 18th century formed a confederacy to protect themselves from the Bugis sultans of Selangor. The name 'Negeri Sembilan' means 'Nine States', and refers to that ancient confederacy. The Minangkabaus brought with them a distinctive architectural style of upswept, high-gabled roofs (representing the horns of a buffalo), a style echoed in several modern buildings in Seremban. A 19th-century, wooden Minangkabau house can be seen at the **Taman Seni Budaya Negeri** (State Art and Culture Park), along with a wooden Minangkabau palace dating from the 1860s. The city's other attractions include the picturesque Lake Gardens (Taman Tasik) and the modernistic Masjid Negeri (State Mosque), whose nine pillars represent Negeri Sembilan's original nine states.

> 🕂 42B2
> **Taman Seni Budaya Negeri**
> ✉ 3km west of city centre, at junction with North–South Highway
> 🕐 Sat, Sun, Tue, Wed 10–6, Thu 8:15–1, Fri 10–12:15, 2:45–6. Closed Mon
> ♿ None
> 🖐 Free

SHAH ALAM ✪

The state capital of Selangor, 30km west of Kuala Lumpur, is a vast, newly developed city of wide freeways, landscaped parks and gleaming modern architecture. It is dominated by the four needle-like minarets and soaring blue dome of the Masjid Sultan Salahuddin Abdul Shah (State Mosque), the largest in the country, capable of accommodating 24,000 worshippers. Nearby are the attractive Lake Gardens and the impressive State Museum.

> 🕂 42B2
> 🍴 Fast-food outlets in PKNS Plaza (£); restaurants in Holiday Inn, Plaza Perangsang, Persiaran Perbandaran (££–£££); Lakeview Floating Restaurant in Lake Gardens (££)
> 🚌 222 from Kelang bus terminal, KL

The country's largest mosque, Masjid Sultan Salahuddin Abdul Shah, in Shah Alam

67

The lovely Lake Gardens of Taiping, laid out in the late 19th century

🔺 42A3
Muzium Perak
✉ Jalan Taming Sari
☎ (05) 847 7757
🕐 Daily 9:30–5. Closed Fri 12:15–2:45
♿ None
🎫 Free

TAIPING ⭐⭐

Formerly known as Larut, this predominantly Chinese town was a rowdy, 19th-century tin-mining centre, riven by feuds among its Triad secret societies. British colonial authorities clamped down on the unrest in 1874 and renamed the town Taiping: 'Everlasting Peace'. Taiping is best-known for having the country's oldest hill station, Maxwell Hill (► 47), and for its Lake Gardens (Taman Tasik), incorporating a small zoo and a 9-hole golf course. **Muzium Perak** is the oldest museum in Malaysia, founded in 1883, and has a collection of natural history exhibits, traditional weapons, musical instruments, and regalia belonging to the sultans of Perak. Upstairs is a display of Orang Asli artefacts, including blow-pipes, weapons, fishing tackle, bird and animal traps, ritual masks and household implements.

🔺 42B2
✉ 1km west of Kuala Selangor
☎ (03) 889 2294
🕐 Daily 9–5
🍴 Cold drinks available (£)
♿ None
🎫 Cheap

TAMAN ALAM KUALA SELANGOR ⭐⭐

This 200-hectare nature reserve near the mouth of the Selangor River protects an area of coastal mangrove forest and secondary jungle, centred around a series of man-made lakes. There are several marked nature trails, a couple of observation towers for bird-watchers, and two board-walks that lead through the mangroves to the coastal mud-flats, where you can see horseshoe crabs and mud-skippers. The secondary jungle, which has grown on drained mangrove swamp, contains troops of macaques and silver leaf monkeys; otters and monitor lizards are occasionally seen in the lakes. The park's main attraction is its bird life: 156 species have been sighted, including herons, egrets, brahminy kites, woodpeckers, kingfishers, bee-eaters, waders and waterfowl. Chalet accommodation is available at the park entrance.

TAMAN NEGARA (► 26, TOP TEN)

TASIK CINI (LAKE CHINI) ✪✪✪

Set in the wilds of southern Pahang, this beautiful lake is said to be inhabited by a giant serpent called Naga Seri Gumum, Malaysia's equivalent of the Loch Ness Monster. Getting to the lake is an adventure in itself: by road to Kampung Belembing on the Pahang River (100km southwest of Kuantan), then by boat along the Cini River, beneath a jungle canopy loud with monkeys and brilliant with butterflies and kingfishers The lake is carpeted with giant lotus plants, whose pink and white flowers bloom between June and September, and fringed with jungle trails and Orang Asli settlements. Accommodation is available in lakeside chalets.

43C2
Lake Chini Resort
☎ (09) 456 7897
🍴 Restuarant at resort (£–££)
♿ None

TEMPLER PARK ✪

Named after its founder, Sir Gerald Templer (Malaya's last British High Commissioner), this 500-hectare forest reserve is criss-crossed by hiking trails which lead past waterfalls, natural swimming pools, picnic sites and caves, overlooked by the 350m limestone peak of Bukit Takun. Although it's not famed for its wildlife, you can expect to see many species of birds and butterflies, and the common silver leaf monkeys.

42B2
✉ Off Highway 1, 20km north of Kuala Lumpur
🕐 Daily, 24 hours
🍴 Hawker stalls at picnic area near entrance (£)
🚌 Bus 66 from KL
♿ None
💰 Free
↔ Batu Caves (➤ 40)

ZOO NEGARA (NATIONAL ZOO) ✪

The 65-hectare National Zoo houses a cross-section of Malaysian wildlife in landscaped enclosures with streams and stands of natural forest centred around a lake. Native species on show include tiger, tapir, honey-bear, water buffalo, crocodile, orang-utan and mouse deer. There are also elephants, giraffes, camels and sea-lions, plus an interesting reptile house and aquarium. Entertainment for children includes daily animal shows and elephant-, camel- and donkey-rides.

42B2
✉ Ulu Kelang, 13km northeast of KL
☎ (03) 408 3422
🕐 Daily 9–5
🍴 Restaurant and hawker stalls (£–££)
🚌 Bus 170, 177
💰 Moderate

69

In the Know

If you only have a short time to visit Malaysia, or would like to get a real flavour of the country, here are some ideas:

10
Ways To Be A Local

Slow Down and take it easy. Away from the cities, life proceeds at a more leisurely pace. Don't be impatient.

Smile! Malaysians are friendly and hospitable, and always greet each other with smiles.

Learn a few words of Bahasa Melayu, even if it's only 'hello', 'please' and 'thank you'. Any attempt to speak the language will be warmly appreciated.

Start the day with a meal of *roti canai* (fried unleavened bread) washed down with sweet, milky coffee.

Dress respectfully when visiting a mosque: arms and legs must be covered and women must wear a headscarf. Take off your shoes before entering.

Be aware of points of social etiquette. The following are considered rude: kissing in public,

raising your voice, touching someone's head (even a child's) and pointing with your finger (Malaysians use a thumb).

Head indoors or seek out some shade during the heat of midday.

Try your hand at the traditional Malaysian pastimes of top-spinning and kite-flying.

Have dinner at a hawker centre, and sample the delights of cheap and tasty local dishes such as *satay* and *char kway teow*.

Have your fortune read by a traditional fortune-teller in Kuala Lumpur's Chinatown.

10
Good Places To Have Lunch

Beijing Riverbank (restaurant ££, café £) ✉ Kuching Waterfront (opposite Hilton Hotel), Sarawak ☎ (082) 234126. Choice of elegant upstairs restaurant

or open-air café, both overlooking the river.

Carcosa Seri Negara Hotel (£££) ✉ Taman Tasik Perdana, Kuala Lumpur ☎ (03) 282 1888. Enjoy a curry tiffin lunch in a splendid colonial villa.

Coliseum Café (£) ✉ 98–100 Jalan Tuanku Abdul Rahman, Kuala Lumpur ☎ (03) 292 6270. Faded décor, but lively atmosphere: a relic of old-time KL.

Eastern and Oriental Hotel (££–£££) ✉ 10 Lebuh Farquhar, George-town, Pulau Pinang ☎ (04) 263 0630. Excellent buffet lunches in elegant, air-conditioned dining room of Pinang's colonial-era hotel.

End of the World (£) ✉ Jalan Hassan Abas, Teluk Bahang, Pulau Pinang ☎ (04) 881 1189. Delicious seafood served beside the jetty where the catch is landed.

Green Planet (£–££) ✉ 63 Jalan Cintra, Georgetown, Pulau Pinang ☎ (04) 261 6192. Stylish and lively coffee-house, popular with travellers, offering good Western and Asian food.

Heeren House (££) ✉ 1 Jalan Tun Tan Cheng Lok, Melaka ☎ (06) 281 4241. Portuguese and Peranakan food in old riverside warehouse.

Seri Angkasa (£££) ✉ Level TH02, Menara KL, Jalan Puncak, Kuala

Lumpur ☎ (03) 208 5055. Fantastic views from this revolving restaurant at the top of 282m KL Tower.

Wishbone Café (££)
✉ 69 Jalan Gaya, Kota Kinabalu, Sabah ☎ (088) 223333. Western and local dishes in quiet and elegant, air-conditioned coffee house.

Ye Olde Smokehouse (££) ✉ Tanah Rata, Cameron Highlands ☎ (05) 491 1215. Cream teas in the rose garden beside this mock-Tudor country hotel.

Above: *Taman Negara transport*
Opposite: *traditional wood-carving in progress*

10
Top Activities

Bird-watching: Malaysian Nature Society ✉ 34 Jalan Bukit Idaman, 8/1 Taman Bukit Idaman, Batu Caves, 68100 Selangor ☎ (03) 616 5259
Golf: Malaysia is a top golf venue (► 114)
Jungle-trekking: Association of Backpackers Malaysia ✉ 6 Jalan SS3/33, 47300 Petaling Jaya, Selangor ☎ (03) 775 6249
Kite-flying: Kelantan State Tourist Information Centre ✉ Jalan Sultan Ibrahim, 15050 Kota Bharu, Kelantan ☎ (09) 748 5534
River safari: Borneo Interland Travel ✉ 63 Main Bazaar, Kuching ☎ (082) 413595 (► 89)
Scuba-diving: Borneo Divers ✉ 4th floor, Wisma Sabah, 8800 Kota Kinabalu, Sabah ☎ (088) 222226

Snorkelling: Terengganu State Tourist Information Centre ✉ Jalan Sultan Zainal Abidin, 20000 Kuala Terengganu ☎ (09) 622 1553
Top-spinning: Kelantan State Tourist Information Centre ✉ Jalan Sultan Ibrahim, 15050 Kota Bharu, Kelantan ☎ (09) 748 5534
Turtle-watching: (► 79)
White-water rafting: Borneo Memories ✉ Second floor, Block B, Asia City Complex, Kota Kinabalu ☎ (088) 255248

10
Best Beaches

- Bunut, Pulau Tioman
- Juara, Pulau Tioman
- Marang
- Pantai Kok, Langkawi
- Pantai Tanjung Rhu, Langkawi
- Pasir Panjang, Pulau Perhentian Kecil
- Pulau Pangkor
- Pulau Rawa
- Tuanku Abdul Rahman National Park, Sabah
- Turtle Islands National Park, Sabah

5
Top Viewpoints

- Bukit Bendera, Pulau Pinang
- Civic Centre, Kuching, Sarawak
- Gunung Brincang, Cameron Highlands
- Menara KL, Kuala Lumpur
- Mount Kinabalu summit, Sabah

5
Famous Hawker Centres

- Gluttons' Corner, Jalan Taman Merdeka, Melaka
- Gurney Drive, George-town, Pulau Pinang
- Jalan Haji Hussein, Chow Kit, Kuala Lumpur
- Pasar Malam, Jalan Padang Garong, Kota Bharu
- Tepian Tebrau, Jalan Abu Bakar, Johor Bahru

71

East Malaysia

The states of Sarawak and Sabah, known together as East Malaysia, cover an area of northern Borneo almost twice the size of Peninsular Malaysia. Separated from the mainland by the South China Sea, this is a vast, wild and adventurous country, where you can climb the highest mountain between New Guinea and the Himalayas, explore the world's largest cave chamber, see the world's largest flower and visit the oldest known human habitation in Southeast Asia. The chief cities of Kuching and Kota Kinabalu serve a hinterland of mountain and forest, home to a range of indigenous peoples, from the former head-hunters of the Iban to the Sea Dayaks and Bajau Laut, the 'sea gypsies' of the Malay Archipelago. Expeditions up the Skrang and Rajang rivers to the longhouses of the Iban of Sarawak are popular excursions from Kuching. In Sabah, if you climb Mount Kinabalu, your guide will be one of the hardy Dusun people.

'Hundreds of butter-flies...floating, flapping ...in small bursts, gliding, fluttering like bats...made their way towards us and settled on our boots and trousers...'

REDMOND O'HANLON
Into the Heart of Borneo (1984)

✚ 29E/F2
Sabah Parks Office
✉ Lot 3, Block K, Kompleks
Sinsuran, Jalan Tun Fuad
Stephens, Kota Kinabalu;
PO Box 10626
☎ (088) 211652
🕓 Mon–Fri 8:30–4:15
(closed Fri 11:30–2), Sat
8:30–noon. Closed Sun

Muzium Sabah
✉ Jalan Muzium, 4km
south of city centre
☎ (088) 253199
🕓 Sat–Thu 10–6 (weekends
and public hols 9–6).
Closed Fri
🍴 Cafeteria (£)
♿ Few
🏛 Free

Sabah

Sabah is known as the 'Land Below the Wind', a name conferred by the pirates of the Sulu Sea because of its location just to the south of the typhoon belt. It is a land of rugged mountains, fringed by coastal swamps and coral islands, bordered to the south by Sarawak and the Indonesian state of Kalimantan.

Rich stocks of tropical hardwood attracted the British North Borneo Company, who administered the territory from 1881 until World War II; after the war North Borneo became a British Crown Colony, and finally joined Malaysia as the state of Sabah in 1963.

Sabah appeals to outdoors enthusiasts, offering superb scuba-diving, jungle-trekking, mountain-climbing and white-water rafting. Its national parks offer rare and exotic wildlife, such as orang-utans, proboscis monkeys, hornbills and *Rafflesia*, the world's largest flower.

Kota Kinabalu, the state capital of Sabah, was originally known as Jesselton, but was renamed after Sabah joined Malaysia in 1963; today it is universally referred to as 'KK'. The city was flattened by bombing during World War II, and the grid of soulless concrete blocks that replaced it has little in the way of character. The main reason for visiting is to arrange trips to one of Sabah's many national parks, either through a tour operator or the Sabah Parks office.

If you have time, it is worth taking a trip out to the **Muzium Sabah** (Sabah Museum), south of the city. The Ethnic Gallery is a good introduction to the cultures of the state's indigenous tribes – the Kadazan, Dusun, Murut and Bajau – and interesting archival photos, documents and newspapers tell the story of Sabah's colonial and wartime history. Less intellectual pursuits are catered for at the golden strand of Tanjung Aru beach, also to the south.

> ### *Did you know ?*
>
> *Mount Kinabalu was the scene of an epic rescue in 1994.
> A British army expedition came to grief
> while attempting the first descent of Low's Gully on
> the north side of the mountain, and five
> team members were airlifted out having survived
> 30 days in the gully.*

Opposite page: *a
medicine man prepares
to advise his patients in
a Sabah market*

SABAH

3

Selat Balabac
Pulau Banggi

Sikuati **Kudat**

Pulau Jambongan

Langkon

Kota Belud
Tuaran Tamparuli Kinabalu
Mengkabong Water Village, National Park
Tunku Abdul Rahman 1101m Kampung Poring Klagan **Turtle Islands**
Kota Kinabalu *Gunung* Hot Springs *Teluk* **National Park**
Tanjung Aru *Kinabalu* Kampung Labuk **Sepilok** **Sandakan**
Kundassang Ranau **Orang-Utan**
Pulau Papar Tambunan **Sanctuary**
Labuan **Gomantong Caves**
Victoria Beaufort Keningau Tomanggong

Tenom Pinangah Lahad Datu
Banjaran Kinabatangan
Maitland Segama
Tomani Banjaran Teluk Lahad Datu
Maligan Brassey Kunak
BRU Long Pa Sia Sigattal Kalabakan **Tawau Hills** Semporna
Kalabakan **National Park**
MAL **RI** **Tawau** ■ **Pulau Sipadan**

0   50   100 km

A   B   C

2

1

What to See in Sabah

GOMANTONG CAVES

✚ 75C2
Wildlife Department
✉ 6th floor, Urusetia Building, Batu 7, Labuk Road (towards Ranau)
☎ (089) 666550
🍴 Picnic site beneath caves, cold drinks (£)
❓ Boat from Sandakan (2 hours), then Land Rover (best by organised tour)
♿ None

These limestone caves, about 32km inland on the far side of the bay from Sandakan (➤ 77), have for centuries been harvested for their swiflets' nests, the raw ingredient of the famous Chinese delicacy, bird's-nest soup. The tiny nests are picked from the cavern roofs by agile collectors, who climb up precariously-rigged bamboo poles and rattan ropes to reach their goal. (The harvesting seasons are February to April and July to September.) There are two caves: Simud Hitam, a 5-minute walk from the Information Centre, soars to height of 90m, and is a source of 'black' nests, which consist of saliva mixed with feathers; and the even larger Simud Putih is reached by an hour's hike up the mountain, and provides the even more valuable white nests, made of pure saliva, and worth around US$500 a kilogram. A permit is necessary, available from the **Wildlife Department** office in Sandakan.

KINABALU NATIONAL PARK (➤ 17)

KUNDASSANG

✚ 75A2

This village, which lies between Ranau and the entrance to Kinabalu National Park, is a market centre for the Kadazan farmers of the surrounding hills. Near by is a memorial to the soldiers who died on the 'Death March' from Sandakan to Ranau in 1945 (➤ 77).

PADAS RIVER

✚ 75A2
Borneo Memories
✉ Lot 11, No.15, 2nd floor, Block B, Asia City Complex, Kota Kinabalu
☎ (088) 255248

The gorge of the Padas River cuts through the southern end of the Crocker Range between the towns of Tenom and Beaufort, and offers an exhilarating expedition for white-water rafters. Trips can be arranged through **Borneo Memories** in Kota Kinabalu.

PORING HOT SPRINGS

✚ 75B2
✉ 19km north of Ranau
⏰ Baths: daily 7AM–6PM; rope-walk: daily 10–4
🍴 Cooking facilities only
🚌 Minibus from Ranau or Kinabalu Park HQ
♿ None
💵 Baths: cheap; free for overnight guests
↔ Kinabalu National Park (➤ 17)

Set in the eastern foothills of Mount Kinabalu, the sulphurous hot springs at Poring are popular with climbers who have just completed an ascent of the mountain. Having soothed your aching muscles in the outdoor hot tubs, built by the Japanese during their World War II occupation, you can take a plunge in the swimming pool, before exploring the surrounding forest. As well as the ordinary hiking trails, there is an exciting rope-walk, suspended in the jungle canopy 30m above ground. Hostel and chalet accommodation must be booked through the Sabah Parks office in Kota Kinabalu (➤ 74).

SANDAKAN ✪

Sandakan was founded in 1879 as a timber town, then in 1884 became the capital of the newly established territory of British North Borneo. The town was occupied by the Japanese during World War II, and completely razed by Allied bombing at the end of the war, after which the capital was transferred to Kota Kinabalu. Sandakan was the starting point of the infamous 'Death March' of early 1945, when 2,400 Australian and British POWs were sent on a 250km forced march to Ranau. Only six men survived – and they had escaped.

The region around Sandakan has for centuries been famous as a source of exotic natural treasures like edible birds' nests, pearls, camphor, sea cucumbers and turtles' eggs, and today it serves as a gateway to the wildlife attractions of Gomantong Caves (► 76), Sepilok Orang-Utan Sanctuary (► 78) and Turtle Islands National Park (► 79) – book at the **Sabah Parks Office**. The town itself has little appeal, save for the colourful fish market, and the Australian War Memorial (12km west on the road to Ranau).

✚ 75C2
Sabah Parks Office
✉ 9th floor, Wisma Khoo Siak Chew, Jalan Buli Sim Sim, Sandakan
☎ (089) 273453
🕐 Mon–Thu 8–12:45, 2–4:15; Fri 8–11:30, 2–4:15; Sat 8–12:45. Closed Sun

Relaxing in the therapeutic waters of Poring Hot Springs

Borneo Divers
✉ 4th floor, Wisma Sabah,
   Kota Kinabalu
☎ (088) 222226

SEMPORNA ✪

This town at the far southeastern frontier of Sabah is built half on land, half on stilts and jetties extending out over the sea. It has a lively seafood market frequented by the local Bajau Laut 'sea-gypsies', but the main reason for visiting is to catch a boat to the marine reserve of Pulau Sipadan, 40km offshore. Sipadan is a world-famous scuba-diving site, a submerged limestone peak capped by a fringing coral reef. On the east side of the island, 'The Wall' drops almost vertically from the surface to a depth of 600m. The waters around Sipadan abound with spectacular marine life, including barracuda, turtles, moray eels, white-tip sharks, whale sharks and a myriad of multi-coloured tropical fish. Trips to the reserve are best organised through dive operators such as **Borneo Divers** in Kota Kinabalu.

Life on the ocean wave: the houses of Semporna are built over the sea

75B2
✉ 25km west of Sandakan
🕐 Sat–Fri 9–12 (Fri 11:30),
   2–4; feeding times 10AM
   and 2PM
🍴 Cafeteria (££)
🚌 Sepilok bus from
   Sandakan, or taxi
♿ None
💰 Expensive

SEPILOK ORANG-UTAN SANCTUARY ✪✪✪

Sabah's best-known wildlife attraction was set up in 1964 to rehabilitate captive and orphaned orang-utans and help them to return to the wild. These red-haired apes are one of humankind's closest living relatives, and are under threat from poachers, logging operations and the disappearance of the rainforest.

The Visitor Information Centre near the park entrance shows videos explaining the main objectives of the sanctuary, but the primary attraction tends to be the feeding platforms. Younger apes are given their twice daily refreshments not far from the Information Centre: older ones call in for their meal of milk and bananas at a platform further out in the forest, a 30-minute hike away. There are a couple of hiking trails through the forest reserve around the sanctuary.

75B1
🍴 Wide range of hawker
   stalls and restaurants (£)
🚌 One bus daily from
   Sandakan (six flights daily
   from Kota Kinabalu)

TAWAU ✪

Tawau is a small but booming commercial port in the wilds of southeastern Sabah, making a living from the export of palm oil, cocoa and timber. An hour's drive to the north is the Tawau Hills National Park, a region of rugged volcanic hills criss-crossed with jungle trails.

Just hanging around: an orang-utan tests the biceps at the Sepilok sanctuary

TUNKU ABDUL RAHMAN NATIONAL PARK ✪✪✪

The five coral islands of this national park lie only a few kilometres off the coast at Kota Kinabalu. They are covered in thick jungle and have beautiful beaches of white coral sand, while the fringing reefs offer excellent snorkelling and scuba-diving. The nearest island, Pulau Gaya, is only 15 minutes by boat from Kota Kinabalu, and all are within reach of a day trip. Chalet accommodation is available on Pulau Manukan and Pulau Mamutik, and camping is allowed on the other islands provided you obtain an official permit; all overnight stays must be arranged through the Sabah Parks Office in Kota Kinabalu.

TURTLE ISLANDS NATIONAL PARK ✪✪✪

A group of tiny coral islands about 40km north of Sandakan is one of the most important nesting grounds for turtles in Southeast Asia. Three of the islands – Pulau Selingan, Pulau Gulisaan and Pulau Bakungan Kecil – were designated as a national park in 1977 to protect the hawksbill and green turtles that crawl ashore to lay their eggs in the white coral sand. Turtles visit the islands all year round, but the peak nesting season for hawksbills is February to April; for green turtles, July to October. Limited accommodation is available on Pulau Selingan, and all visits must be organised through the Sabah Parks offices in Sandakan or Kota Kinabalu. Day trips are not possible.

Sabah Parks Office
⊠ Lot 3, Block K, Kompleks
   Sinsuran, Jalan Tun Fuad
   Stephens, Kota Kinabalu
☎ (088) 211652
⏲ Mon–Fri 8:30–4:15
   (closed Fri 11:30–2), Sat
   8:30–noon. Closed Sun

✚ 75A2
🍴 Restaurant on Pulau
   Manukan (£)
⛴ Ferry service from jetty
   below Hyatt Hotel
♿ None
🎟 Park admission: cheap

✚ 75C2
🍴 Restaurant on Pulau
   Selingan (£)
⛴ Organised boat trips only
♿ None

Food & Drink

One of the main attractions of a holiday in Malaysia is the opportunity to sample a wide range of delicious and exotic dishes, which are sold at ridiculously low prices.

Malay

Malaysian cuisine has been influenced by contact with the cultures of Thailand, China, Indonesia, India, the Middle East and Portugal, but it is still based firmly on local produce: fish, beef, chicken, rice, coconut, peanuts, lime juice, chillis, tamarind, spices and a fermented fish sauce called *sambal belacan*. The national dish, available at almost every hawker centre, is *satay*, tiny kebabs of chicken or beef, marinated in lime juice and soy sauce, and barbecued over glowing coals, served with a spicy peanut sauce. Rice (*nasi*) can be steamed in a palm-leaf parcel, or cooked in coconut milk (*nasi lemak*) or fried (*nasi goreng*), and is usually accompanied by egg, peanuts and cucumber, and garnished with crunchy, deep-fried anchovies (*ikan bilis*). Fish is very popular, and is usually grilled whole (*ikan bakar*), while beef and chicken are often served in spicy, coconut curry sauce like *rendang* or *percik*. A classic dish from Pinang is *laksa*, a rich, spicy soup made with prawns, *belacan* and bean-sprouts thickened with rice noodles; a Peranakan variation from Melaka (*laksa lemak*) is flavoured with coconut cream. A meal at a hawker centre can be washed down with soy-bean milk, sugar-cane syrup, or freshly prepared tropical fruit juice – lime, pineapple, mango, starfruit, papaya, guava – or the unusual Malaysian dessert called *ais kacang*: a cocktail of shaved ice, syrup, condensed milk, jelly cubes and beans.

Mouth-watering snacks on offer at a Kuala Lumpur street stall

Indian

Malaysia's Indian community originated largely in the south of the country, where the Hindu Tamil food is strictly vegetarian. Vegetable curries are served on banana-leaf 'plates', accompanied by a mound of steamed rice, and

eaten using the fingers of the right hand. Northern Indian cuisine is usually served in more expensive restaurants, and is based on chicken and lamb, marinated in yoghurt and spices, and cooked in a clay oven called a *tandoor*. Such *tandoori* meals are accompanied by breads such as *naan*, *paratha* and *chapati* cooked in the *tandoor*.

Delicious and cheap Indian snacks include *murtabak*, a 'pancake' of paper-thin bread dough stuffed with egg and a choice of meat or vegetables; *samosa*, a pastry parcel of spicy meat and/or vegetables, and *roti canai*, a popular breakfast dish of lightly fried *murtabak* dough with a bowl of *dahl* (spiced lentils) or curry gravy as a dip.

Above: a pick-and-mix tray of Malaysian food in Georgetown

Below: good food and good company make for a special occasion at a Chinese restaurant

Chinese

Chinese food can be found all over Malaysia, but especially in the cities of the west coast and in Kuching. There are many regional variations, from the Cantonese and Beijing cuisines familiar in the West to the less well-known specialities of Sichuan, Hainan, Hokkien and Teochew. Classic Chinese hawker dishes include Hainan chicken-rice, which is as simple as it is delicious: steamed or fried chicken served with a clear chicken soup, steamed rice and vegetables, with ginger and chilli sauce on the side; and *char kway teow*: fried flat noodles with prawns or meat, vegetables and a spicy sauce.

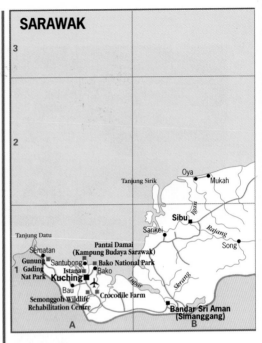

Sarawak

Sarawak is Malaysia's largest state, occupying an area of northwestern Borneo that is almost the size of England, but with a population of only 1.5 million. It is bordered to the south and east by the Indonesian state of Kalimantan, and to the north by Sabah and the tiny, oil-rich kingdom of Brunei.

Sarawak was once a province of the sultanate of Brunei, but in 1841 the sultan rewarded the English adventurer James Brooke for his help in suppressing a revolt by making him the Rajah of Sarawak. Brooke and his descendants ruled Sarawak as the famous 'White Rajahs' until World War II, after which the territory was ceded to the British crown, before finally joining the Federation of Malaysia in 1963.

Kuching, the state capital of Sarawak, is one of Malaysia's most interesting and enjoyable cities, with an attractive waterfront, colourful streets and the country's best museum (▶ 19). The Malay word *kucing* means 'cat', a fact celebrated by a number of cat sculptures scattered across the city, but the name probably derives either from the Chinese word *kochin*, meaning 'harbour', or from the *mata kucing* tree (the 'cat's eye' fruit) which is

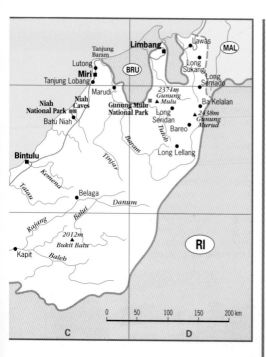

widespread along the river banks. Although there are good roads around Kuching, the boat remains the most important form of transport in Sarawak, both along the coast and inland up the many navigable rivers. The main attractions for visitors are the spectacular national parks of Bako, Gunung Mulu and the Niah Caves, and the opportunity to journey upriver and visit traditional Iban longhouses.

Boats on the Sarawak River, near Kuching

What to See in Kuching

CHINESE HISTORY MUSEUM

This little museum, on the waterfront opposite the Tua Pek Tong temple, charts the history of Sarawak's sizeable Chinese community, from the days of the earliest traders through the Brooke period and into modern times.

📍 82A1
✉ Main Bazaar
🕐 Tue–Sun 9–6. Closed Mon
💷 Free

CIVIC CENTRE TOWER ✪✪

This futuristic, umbrella-roofed tower sits on a hilltop south of the city centre. Take the lift to the viewing terrace at the top for a magnificent view across the city and the river to the peaks of Gunung Santubong and Gunung Matang. To the south, on a clear day, you can see the mountain ranges of the interior along the border with Kalimantan.

📍 82A1
✉ Jalan Budaya
🕐 Daily 9–6
🍴 Restaurant and cafeteria at top (££)
💷 Free

FORT MARGHERITA

A *tampang* (ferry) will take you across the river from the steps below the Square Tower to visit this relic of the White Rajahs. The fort was built in 1879 to guard the river against pirates, and was named after Margaret, the wife of the second rajah, Charles Brooke. A Police Museum has weapons and uniforms, and relics of the Japanese occupation. The fort is in the grounds of a barracks and you may be asked for identification at the entrance: take your passport. Upstream from the fort, on the same bank, is the Istana, an elegant palace built for Charles Brooke in 1870 and now the official residence of Sarawak's head of state.

📍 82A1
🕐 Tue–Sun 10–6. Closed Mon and public hols
⛴ Ferry from steps below Square Tower
♿ None
💷 Free

Above: *the striking white stone of Fort Margherita gleams above the trees*

MASJID KUCHING

The golden onion-domes of the Kuching Mosque dominate the west end of the city centre, and look especially impressive when seen from the river. Built in 1968 on the site of a wooden 19th-century mosque, this was the state mosque until that distinction was bestowed on a new building across the river at Petra Jaya. Visitors must be suitably dressed (► 70).

82A1

✉ Jalan Mosque

⏰ Closed to non-Muslims Sat 4–6, Sun 2–5, and 3PM Thu–3PM Fri

SARAWAK MUSEUM

Kuching is fortunate to have what is probably the richest and most varied museum collection in Malaysia, if not in the whole of Southeast Asia. The collection is shared between two buildings. The Old Building, opened in 1891, houses an extensive natural history exhibition, which includes many items collected during the 19th century under the direction of British naturalist Alfred Russell Wallace. It also has a magnificent ethnographic collection, which includes a reconstruction of an Iban longhouse complete with shrunken heads bagged by the Iban tribes-people.

A footbridge leads over the road to the New Building, which has more ethnographic exhibits, a display of Chinese ceramics, and a re-creation of one of the Niah Caves. There is also a good bookshop and souvenir store. The grounds behind the old building contain botanical gardens and an aquarium.

82A1

✉ Jalan Tun Haji Openg

☎ (082) 244232

⏰ Sat–Thu 9–6. Closed Fri

♿ None

🎫 Free

TUA PEK KONG

Kuching's oldest Chinese temple dates from the 1840s, and is probably the oldest surviving building in the city. It is brightly decorated, with red walls and green steps guarded by blue and gold ceramic dragons, and there is always a handful of devotees lighting joss-sticks or burning paper money and making invocations to Loh Hong Pek, the resident deity.

82A1

✉ Corner of Jalan Tunku Abdul Rahman and Jalan Padungan

⏰ Early morning–late evening

Did you know ?

The British naturalist Alfred Russell Wallace (1823–1913), while travelling and collecting in the Malay Archipelago in the 1850s, arrived at a theory of evolution by natural selection independently of Charles Darwin. It was Russell who first coined the term 'survival of the fittest'.

A Walk Around Kuching

Distance
3km

Time
1 hr, not including time spent
visiting attractions

Start point
Visitors' Information Centre,
Padang Merdeka
🔁 82A1

End point
Sarawak Museum
🔁 82A1

Lunch
Travellers' Corner Café (£)
✉ Kuching Waterfront
☎ (082) 234126

Mosques, temples and markets feature in this walk, which
also visits the city's new waterfront.

*From the Visitors' Information Centre go left
along the side of the Padang, and turn first
left along Jalan Mosque. Continue towards the
golden domes of the Masjid Kuching (▶ 85),
and turn right in front of the mosque. Follow
this street past the Brooke Shipyard and along
an arcade of shophouses on the left. At the end
of the shops, cross the road and head right.*

Market stalls and warehouses line the riverbank, as the
route passes the fish and vegetable markets, to reach the
beginning of the new waterfront at the Square Tower, a
tiny fort built in 1879. On the right is the 19th-century
Court House and a memorial to Rajah Charles Brooke.

*Stroll along the
Esplanade.*

There are views across the river
of the Istana and Fort
Margherita (▶ 84); the
Esplanade ends at the Beijing
Riverside restaurant and
Travellers' Corner café.

Kuching's market is full
of wonderfully fresh
produce

*Return along the
waterfront as far as the
bend in the river, and go
left through the gardens
to the Chinese History Museum. Cross the main
road near the colourful Tua Pek Tong temple
and turn right along a row of shophouses, then
left along Lebuh Wayang for one block to
another Chinese temple on the right. Turn
right at this temple along Jalan Ewe Hai and
its continuation Jalan Carpenter. At the far
end turn left opposite the Court House.*

Having led through the heart of Chinatown, the route
passes the grand Corinthian façade of the Post Office to
reach the open, grassy expanse of Padang.

The museum is just ahead on the left.

What to See in Sarawak

BAKO NATIONAL PARK ✪✪✪

The remarkable sandstone sea cliffs and fascinating jungle trails of Bako National Park are easily accessible from Kuching. Chalets, a hostel and a campsite provide accommodation near the beach at Teluk Assam; permits are needed for visits to the park; these and accommodation reservations can be arranged at the **Visitors' Information Centre** in Kuching.

82A1
Visitors' Information Centre
⊠ Padang Merdeka, Kuching
☎ (082) 410944
🕐 Mon–Thu 8–4:15, Fri 8–4:45, Sat 8–12:45. Closed Sun

GUNUNG GADING NATIONAL PARK ✪✪

This nature reserve, a two-hour drive west of Kuching, is home to many species of rare plants, including the spectacular earth-star, or *Rafflesia*, the world's largest flower. It gained its name after Sir Thomas Stamford Raffles, the founder of Singapore, was the first to record a description of this remarkable plant. The *Rafflesia* is a parasite, growing on the roots of forest vines, and the plant's body is invisible, a mere network of thin strands penetrating the body of its host. The flower, however, is up to one metre across, weighs up to 10kg and smells like rotting meat, attracting the carrion flies which act as pollinating agents. It lasts only a few days after blooming. Board-walks lead from the park's information centre to known *Rafflesia* habitats, but seeing a fully developed flower is matter of luck. It is best to telephone park HQ first, to find out if any are in bloom.

82A1
⊠ Near Lundu, about 70km west of Kuching
☎ Park HQ: (082) 735714

The coastline at Bako National Park is spectacular

83D2
National Parks and Wildlife Office
✉ Forest Department, Wisma Sumber Alam, Petra Jaya, Kuching
☎ (082) 442180

GUNUNG MULU NATIONAL PARK   ✪✪✪

The most spectacular of Sarawak's natural wonders lies on the flanks of the 2,736m peak of Gunung Mulu, 100km east of Miri. Here a thick band of limestone conceals a cave system which includes the world's largest cave chamber – the 700m by 400m Sarawak Chamber, discovered in 1980. It ranges in height from 70m to over 110m – big enough to hold 48 football fields, and tall enough to accommodate the Statue of Liberty with room to spare. The Deer Cave, an hour's walk from park HQ, has a huge colony of bats, which emerge in a swirling cloud each evening around dusk. A 10-minute boat trip leads to the Clearwater Cave, which has a plank-walk alongside the underground river leading to impressive limestone formations. The Sarawak Chamber can only be visited on an organised adventure caving trip. Above ground, the park offers a three-day trek to see The Pinnacles, a 'forest' of razor-sharp, 50m limestone pinnacles emerging from the jungle, or a four-day hike to the summit of Gunung Mulu and back. It is easiest to visit the park as part of an organised tour, and at least two or three days are necessary to make the trip worthwhile. A range of accommodation is available at the park headquarters.

Right: *children peering down from their longhouse*

Far right: *morning wash down at the river*

MIRI ✪

Oil money has made Miri the biggest and brashest town in Sarawak, and its population of oil workers on leave from the rigs gives it a lively, cosmopolitan atmosphere. The city has many good restaurants and an attractive beach, but most travellers use it as a base for exploring the Niah Caves and Gunung Mulu national parks.

NIAH NATIONAL PARK (► 21, TOP TEN)

RIVER SAFARIS ✪✪

For centuries the Rajang River and its tributaries have served as a natural highway into the interior of Sarawak. Overland travel is difficult in this land of thick jungle, mountain and swamp, and boats have always been the major form of transport, from the traditional canoes of the Iban people (now propelled by outboard motors) to the seagoing coasters that trade upriver as far as Sibu. Regular ferries ply from Sibu upstream to Kapit, the starting point for expeditions to Iban longhouses. Official permits are necessary for such trips, and boats and boatmen must be hired, so it is best to take an organised tour. These generally depart from Sibu, and last from two to four days.

➕ 83C3
Visitors' Information Centre
✉ 452 Jalan Melayu
☎ (085) 434181
🕐 Mon–Thu 8–4:15, Fri 8–4:45, Sat 8–12:45. Closed Sun

➕ 82A1 for Kuching departure
➕ 83B1 for Sibu departure

Borneo Interland Travel
✉ 63 Main Bazaar, Kuching
☎ (082) 413595

Dayak paintings on show at the Cultural Village

SANTUBONG

Kuching's nearest beach is near the fishing village of Santubong, set at the mouth of a river below the peak of Gunung Santubong. Rock carvings found near by are thought to belong to an ancient trading settlement mysteriously abandoned in the 14th century. A scenic coastal road leads north from Santubong to the beach resort of Pantai Damai and the **Kampung Budaya Sarawak** (Sarawak Cultural Village), a showcase for the state's diversity of traditional cultures. The village contains replicas of the traditional huts and longhouses of the Iban, Orang Ulu, Melanau and Penan peoples, as well as typical Malay and Chinese dwellings, each housing a display of crafts belonging to the various cultures.

SIBU ✪

Sibu is a working port and service centre for the logging industry. Timber is sent by boat down the 'Rajang Highway' and transferred to sea-going ships, which can navigate as far as Sibu, 60km from the open sea. Most travellers pass through on their way upriver to the Iban longhouses of the interior (see River Safaris, ➤ 89). The city has a wide selection of hotels and restaurants.

SEMENGGOH WILDLIFE REHABILITATION CENTRE ✪✪

This 740-hectare forest reserve is Sarawak's equivalent of the famous Sepilok Orang-Utan Sanctuary in Sabah. Here orang-utans, honey-bears, hornbills and other native animals which have been orphaned, injured, or recovered from poachers are nursed back to health and prepared for a return to the wild. You can watch the semi-wild orang-utans enjoy their daily feed, and stroll along the board-walk for a closer look at the tropical forest. Permits should be obtained at the Visitors' Centre in Kuching.

Where To...

Peninsular Malaysia

Prices

Prices are approximate, based on a three-course meal for one without drinks and service:

£ = under RM15
££ = RM15–40
£££ = over RM40

Hawker Cuisine

Some of the tastiest food in Malaysia can be enjoyed at a hawkers' centre: a gathering of dozens of tiny cooking stalls, each specialising in a single dish. Choose a seat at the communal tables, then wander around the stalls and order a selection of dishes; the cooks will be only too happy to explain the ingredients and preparation. You pay each cook separately when the food arrives at your table; other hawkers will come to take orders for drinks.

Kuala Lumpur

American Chilli's (££)
A Tex-Mex grill offering steaks, burgers, chilli and nachos.
✉ Shazan Tower, Jalan Raja Culan ☎ (03) 248 1400 🕐 Lunch, dinner

Bangles (££)
An up-market Indian restaurant specialising in Moghul cuisine of northern India.
✉ 60 Jalan Tuanku Abdul Rahman ☎ (03) 298 3780 🕐 Lunch, dinner

Bilal (££)
For spice-lovers: super-hot curry dishes from southern India, served in a pleasant setting.
✉ 33 Jalan Ampang ☎ (03) 232 0804 🕐 Lunch, dinner

Café Le Parc (££–£££)
Despite the French name, this is actually one of the city's premier Italian restaurants.
✉ 3rd floor, City Square Centre, Jalan Tun Razak ☎ (03) 273 3140 🕐 Lunch, dinner

Central Market (£)
The first and second floors of the market building are devoted to hawker stalls offering Malay, Chinese and Indian specialities at bargain prices.
✉ Jalan Hang Kasturi 🕐 10AM–10PM

Chinatown (£)
A wide range of superb Chinese dishes is served at these hawker stalls, set out in a maze of wooden walkways which can be reached via narrow alleys from either street.
✉ Jalan Petaling and Jalan Tun HS Lee 🕐 All day. Closes 7PM

Coliseum Café (£–££)
Faded relic of old-time Kuala Lumpur, with lively bar. Famous for its sizzling steaks. European and Asian cuisine.
✉ Coliseum Hotel, 98–100 Jalan Tuanku Abdul Rahman ☎ (03) 292 6270 🕐 Lunch, dinner

Dondang Sayang (££)
This restaurant specialises in traditional Malay dishes, including the Nyonya cuisine of Melaka.
✉ Life Centre, 99 Jalan Sultan Ismail ☎ (03) 264 6188 🕐 Lunch, dinner

Golden Triangle hawker centre (£)
You can find excellent Chinese noodle dishes, chicken rice and grilled fish (ikan bakar) in Jalan Alor (behind the Sungai Wang Hotel), and Malay and Indian food in Jalan Perak (near the Hilton Hotel).
✉ Jalan Alor and Jalan Perak 🕐 7PM till late

Kapitan's Club (££)
Atmospheric restaurant set in a restored shophouse, and specialising in Peranakan cuisine.
✉ 35 Jalan Ampang ☎ (03) 201 0242 🕐 Lunch, dinner

Le Coq d'Or (£££)
Sophisticated international cuisine at the upper end of the price range, served in the palatial setting of an old colonial mansion once owned by a tin millionaire.
✉ 12 Jalan Ampang ☎ (03) 261 9732 🕐 Lunch, dinner

Nelayan Floating Restaurant (££)

A picturesque, *kampung-*style restaurant set on a lakeside, offering a selection of Chinese, Malay and seafood dishes.

✉ Taman Tasik Titiwangsa, Jalan Temerloh (off Jalan Pahang) ☎ (03) 422 8400 🕐 Lunch, dinner

Rasa Utara (££)

Sit in the comfort of a modern, air-conditioned restaurant and enjoy Malay dishes from the Kedah region.

✉ Bukit Bintang Plaza, Jalan Bukit Bintang ☎ (03) 248 8369 🕐 Lunch, dinner

Riverbank (£)

Pleasant café-bar with terrace overlooking river. Steaks, burgers and sandwiches, plus Chinese fish and noodle dishes.

✉ Ground Floor, Central Market, Jalan Hang Kasturi ☎ (03) 274 6652 🕐 Lunch, dinner

Satay Station (££)

This is a rather up-market, air-conditioned alternative to the traditional hawker centres, with a range of hawker specialities.

✉ Holiday Inn on the Park, Jalan Pinang ☎ (03) 248 1066 🕐 Lunch, dinner

Scalini's (£££)

Trendy and elegant Italian restaurant, set right in the heart of the city's Golden Triangle.

✉ 19 Jalan Sultan Ismail ☎ (03) 245 3211 🕐 Dinner

Seri Angkasa (£££)

Revolving restaurant with great views from the top of the 282m KL Tower; it completes its 360° revolution every 52 minutes.

✉ Level TH02, Menara KL, Jalan Puncak ☎ (03) 208 5055 🕐 Lunch, dinner

Seri Malaysia (££)

Come here for food and entertainment: traditional Malay cuisine, accompanied by performances of traditional music and dance.

✉ 1 Jalan Conlay ☎ (03) 241 4699 🕐 Dinner

Shang Palace (£££)

One of Kuala Lumpur's top Chinese restaurants, with luxurious dining room and superb food. Noted for its *dim-sum*.

✉ Shangri-La Hotel, Jalan Sultan Ismail ☎ (03) 232 2388 🕐 Lunch, dinner

The Ship (££)

One of a chain of trendy western, pub-style restaurants, offering steaks, grills and seafood.

✉ 40–1/40–2 Jalan Sultan Ismail ☎ (03) 241 8805 🕐 Lunch, dinner

Teochew (££)

An excellent Chinese restaurant which has an enormous selection of dishes on offer.

✉ 270–272 Jalan Cangkat Thambi Dollah (off Jalan Pudu) ☎ (03) 241 5851 🕐 Lunch, dinner

TGI Friday (££)

American-style grill serving steaks, burgers, pizza and pasta; part of the well-known chain. Adjoining pub and disco.

✉ Life Centre, 99–100 Jalan Sultan Ismail ☎ (03)263 7761 🕐 Dinner

Tea

Tea-growing was introduced to Malaysia in 1929, when John Archibald Russell established the Boh Tea Estate in the Cameron Highlands. The estate still operates today, producing 3.7 million kg of tea each year; the processing plant at the Sungai Palas branch is open to the public. The estate specialises in the production of Assam, a fully fermented black tea that originates in Inda.

Big Ones, Small Ones ...

Coconut is a staple ingredient of Malay cuisine. The fresh flesh and milk are blended into a smooth cream that cools and complements the often fiery flavours of chilli and *galanggal* (a hot, ginger-like root), and the milk is also used to cook 'sticky rice', or *nasi lemak*. The juice of unripe nuts makes a sweet and refreshing drink.

Cameron Highlands

Orient (£)

Chinese restaurant. A particularly good place to try out the local 'steamboat' speciality.

✉ **Jalan Besar** 🕐 **Lunch, dinner**

Thanam (£)

A low-cost Indian restaurant with outdoor tables, serving a tasty menu of various curries, claypot rice and *murtabak*.

✉ **Jalan Besar, Tanah Rata** 🕐 **Lunch, dinner**

Ye Olde Smokehouse (££)

Mock-Tudor hotel, established in 1937 and offering a menu of British favourites, including the obligatory cream teas in the garden.

✉ **2km beyond Tanah Rata** ☎ **(05) 491 1215** 🕐 **Lunch, dinner**

Johor Bahru

East and West (£)

A bright and cheerful restaurant, which lives up to its name with a selection of good-value local specialities as well as some Western dishes such as steak and chips.

✉ **5th floor, Plaza Kota Raya, Jalan Trus** ☎ **(07) 222 9728** 🕐 **Lunch, dinner**

Kukup (££)

This is a popular outing for locals and Singaporeans, and a novelty for tourists. Waterside 'village on stilts' specialising in dishes that include steamed fish, prawns, lobsters, crabs and chilli mussels.

✉ **Kukup Laut (on coast 40km southwest of JB)** 🕐 **Lunch, dinner**

Marina Seafood Village (££)

Large and popular seafood restaurant offering great quality and variety in its dishes.

✉ **Jalan Skudai, 3km west of city centre** ☎ **(07) 224 1400** 🕐 **Lunch, dinner**

Pasar Malam (night market) (£)

Bustling outdoor hawker centre overlooked by a Hindu temple. The accent here is on *ikan bakar* (grilled fish) and other varieties of seafood.

✉ **Jalan Wong Ah Fook** 🕐 **Dinner**

Sedap Corner (£–££)

Good value selection of Malay, Chinese and Thai food, including traditional fish-head curry.

✉ **11 Jalan Abdul Samad** ☎ **(07) 224 6566** 🕐 **Breakfast, lunch, dinner**

Kota Bharu

Pasar Malam (night market) (£)

Hawker stalls offer a wide range of dishes, including local specialities such as the Thai-influenced *ayam percik* (barbecued chicken with green curry sauce), *keropok batang* (fish sausages served with chilli dipping sauce) and *nasi kerabu* (coloured rice served with coconut and seaweed).

✉ **Jalan Padang Garong** 🕐 **Dinner**

Kuala Terengganu

Afzal Tandoori (££)

Indian restaurant dishing up classic curries, *biryanis* and delicious *nan* bread, plus a few less common offerings such as fried quail.

✉ **27 Jalan Sultan Mahmud**
☎ (09) 623 2913 🕐 **Breakfast, lunch, dinner**

Batu Buruk Food Centre (£)
Collection of Malay and Chinese food stalls, set out under a covered pavilion at the southern end of the city beach.
✉ **Jalan Persinggahan (off Jalan Sultan Mahmud)**
🕐 **Dinner**

Good Luck (££)
Enjoy some fine Chinese food, and enjoy your meal sitting at a pleasant outdoor table.
✉ **11 Jalan Kota Lama** ☎ (09) 622 7573 🕐 **Lunch, dinner**

Kuantan
Riverside Hawker Centre (£)
A selection of outdoor stalls serving a range of seafood and Malay specialities, and set in a pleasant riverbank location.
✉ **Jalan Besar** 🕐 **Dinner**

Thomson Steak House (££)
The good Western-style menu includes such staple items as fish and chips and juicy tenderloin steaks, which are flown in to the country all the way from New Zealand.
✉ **65 Jalan Telok Sisek**
☎ (09) 552792 🕐 **Dinner**

Marang
Marang Guest House and Restaurant (£)
An attractive terrace restaurant with a wonderful view over the palm-fringed lagoon to the island of Kapas.
✉ **Main Street, Marang**
☎ (09) 618 9176 🕐 **Lunch, dinner**

Melaka
Banana Leaf (£)
Southern Indian vegetarian meals, beautifully presented on a 'plate' fashioned from a banana leaf.
✉ **42 Jalan Munshi Abdullah**
☎ (06) 283 2607 🕐 **Breakfast, lunch, dinner**

Bob's Tavern (££)
English-style pub serving steaks and, of course, fish and chips (made with beer batter).
✉ **19–21 Lorong Hang Jebat**
☎ (06) 282 2886 🕐 **Lunch, dinner**

Glutton's Corner (£)
Long-established hawker centre serving an interesting range of Malay, Chinese and Indian fare, including excellent *roti canai* breakfasts, and spicy beef and chicken *satay*.
✉ **Jalan Taman Merdeka**
🕐 **Breakfast, lunch, dinner**

Heeren House (££)
Attractive café in a small hotel which overlooks the river. Serves mostly Portuguese and Peranakan cuisine, with some Western dishes.
✉ **1 Jalan Tun Tan Cheng Lock**
☎ (06) 281 4241 🕐 **Breakfast, lunch, dinner**

Makhota Parade Food Centre (£)
Air-conditioned, indoor alternative to Glutton's Corner in a vast, new shopping centre that also houses Western fast-food outlets, including big names like McDonald's, Dunkin Donuts, A & W and Burger King.
✉ **Jalan Taman Merdeka**
🕐 **Lunch, dinner**

Fruity Treats
A bewildering variety of tropical fruits can be enjoyed in Malaysia, from bananas, pineapples and mangoes to more exotic delights such as starfruit (yellow, crisp and refreshing), rambutan (small red and 'hairy', concealing a pale flesh that tastes like lychee) and durian (the 'king of fruits', huge, green and spiky, with a foul-smelling flesh that is definitely an acquired taste).

95

Combined Cultures

Peranakan means 'intermarriage' and refers to the Straits Chinese community who flourished in Melaka in the 19th century and intermarried with local Malay women. The blending of cultures is evident in Peranakan (also known as Nyonya) cuisine, which combines Chinese ingredients and cooking techniques with Malay spices and flavourings like coconut and lemon grass to produce a unique and intriguing result.

Manis Sayang (££)

Bright and busy Peranakan restaurant, which offers a wide-ranging menu at mid-range prices.

✉ 617–618 Taman Melaka Raya ☎ (06) 281 3393
🕐 Lunch, dinner

Nyonya Makko (££)

Up-market Peranakan restaurant set on the busy nightlife strip to the east of the city centre.

✉ 123 Jalan Taman Melaka Raya ☎ (06) 284 0737
🕐 Lunch, dinner

Ole Sayang (££)

A Peranakan restaurant complete with restored traditional décor.

✉ 199 Jalan Taman Melaka Raya ☎ (06) 283 1366
🕐 Lunch, dinner

Pandan (£)

Malay and Western food served in this shady garden café beside the river. Conveniently located just behind the tourist information office.

✉ Jalan Quayside
🕐 Breakfast, lunch, dinner

Peranakan (££)

Opulent Peranakan villa with a garden courtyard serving delicious Peranakan dishes. Cultural shows are presented in the evenings.

✉ 317C Jalan Klebang Besar (7km north on road to Port Dickson) ☎ (06) 385 4436

Restoran de Lisbon (£)

Fresh seafood cooked Portuguese/Malay style in open courtyard beside the sea.

✉ Medan Portugis (3km east of city centre) ☎ (06) 284 8067
🕐 Dinner

Pulau Langkawi
Backofen (££)

Austrian-style coffee house serving European food, as well as local dishes, pizza, pastries and Viennese coffee.

✉ Pantai Cenang ☎ (04) 955 1667 🕐 Breakfast, lunch, dinner

Champor-Champor (££)

Elegant eating place offering a mix of Malay and European cuisine.

✉ Pantai Cenang ☎ (04) 955 1449 🕐 Lunch, dinner

Domino (££)

A bright, modern restaurant and coffee shop which offers a menu of steaks, burgers, ice cream and Brazilian coffee.

✉ Jalan Pandak Mayah 6, Kuah ☎ (04) 966 7214
🕐 Lunch, dinner

Hajjah (££)

Good Malay seafood restaurant specialising in fish-head curry, prawn *sambal*, cuttlefish and steamed crab.

✉ Kampung Kelibana ☎ (04) 966 8070 🕐 Lunch, dinner

Spice Market (££)

Up-market Malay and Asian cuisine served up in this beautiful restaurant with a lovely setting, overlooking the beach.

✉ Pelangi Beach Resort, Pantai Cenang ☎ (04) 955 1001
🕐 Lunch, dinner

Pulau Pinang
Dawood (££)

Established in 1947, Dawood serves authentic southern Indian cuisine and non-alcoholic drinks.

✉ 63 Lebuh Queen,

Georgetown ☎ (04) 261 1633
🕐 Lunch, dinner

Eden Seafood Village (££)
This lively Chinese restaurant offers regular evening entertainment along with the meals; specialises in seafood.
✉ 69A Batu Feringgi ☎ (04) 881 1852 🕐 Lunch, dinner

Gurney Drive hawker centre (£)
Outdoor tables are set out next to the waterfront, with stalls offering dishes such as satay, char kway teow, laksa, nasi ayam, sotong (cuttlefish) and other traditional favourites.
✉ Pesiaran Gurney, Bagan Jermal 🕐 Dinner

Hot Wok Café (££)
Old-style coffee-shop equipped with marble tables and antiques, serving traditional Pinang and Nyonya dishes such as Curry Kapitan and otak-otak.
✉ 125D Jalan Tanjung Tokong, Desa Tanjung ☎ (04) 899 0858 🕐 Lunch, dinner

Istana (££)
A theatre-restaurant, where your meal of classic Malay cuisine will be accompanied by a performance of traditional music and dancing.
✉ Pinang Cultural Centre, Jalan Hassan Abbas, Teluk Bahang ☎ (04) 885 1175 🕐 Dinner

Komtar Food Court (£)
A pleasant, indoor hawker centre, which has over 60 stalls, offering a variety of food – Malay, Chinese, Indian, Thai and Indonesian dishes.

✉ Fifth floor, Kompleks Tuanku Abdul Razak (Komtar), Jalan Pinang 🕐 Breakfast, lunch, dinner

Kurumaya (££)
This Japanese restaurant has a relaxed atmosphere, and offers dishes such as teppanyaki and sushi flown in fresh from Japan.
✉ 269 Jalan Burma, Georgetown ☎ (04) 228 3222 🕐 Lunch, dinner

Tandoori House (££)
Authentic Moghul curry dishes from northern India are served up in a comfortable, air-conditioned dining room.
✉ 36 Lorong Hutton, Georgetown ☎ (04) 261 9105 🕐 Lunch, dinner

Tower Palace (££)
Quality Chinese restaurant at the top of the Komtar Tower. Superb views over Georgetown.
✉ 60th Floor, Komtar Tower, Kompleks Tuanku Abdul Razak, Jalan Pinang ☎ (04) 262 2222 🕐 Lunch, dinner

20 Leith Street (££–£££)
This stylish bistro and wine bar has been set in a beautifully restored Chinese shophouse.
✉ 20 Lebuh Leith, Georgetown ☎ (04) 261 8573 🕐 Dinner

The View (££)
Pinang's best Italian restaurant, and one of Malaysia's top 100, with great panoramic views over the south of the island. Located near the airport.
✉ Hotel Equatorial Penang, 1 Jalan Bukit Jambul, Bayan Lepas ☎ (04) 643 8111 🕐 Lunch, dinner

Juices
Fruit juice is an ideal way to quench a tropical thirst, and can be bought, freshly squeezed, from street stalls and hawker centres. Lime, orange, papaya, guava and starfruit juice are all popular, but you will also see sugar-cane syrup (a sweet, green syrup extracted using a hand-cranked mangle) and soya-bean milk.

East Malaysia

Best Nests

For centuries past the people of Sabah and Sarawak have harvested the limestone caves of Borneo for the nests of swiftlets, the prized ingredient of that famous Chinese delicacy, bird's nest soup. The nests, made from the birds' congealed saliva, are made into a gelatinous broth which is said to cure breathing problems and improve the complexion.

Kota Kinabalu

Nan Xing (£–££)

A pleasant Chinese restaurant specialising in Cantonese cuisine, including *dim-sum*, as well as steaks and chops.

✉ 33–35 Jalan Haji Saman ☎ (088) 212900 ⏰ Lunch, dinner

New Arafat (£)

Basic eatery serving Indian Muslim food, including delicious *roti canai* breakfasts.

✉ Block I, Sinsuran Kompleks, Jalan Pasar Baru ☎ None ⏰ 24 hours

Phoenix Court (£££)

Stylish and expensive Chinese restaurant offering Cantonese and Szechuan specialities.

✉ Hyatt Kinabalu International, Jalan Datuk Salleh Sulong ☎ (088) 221234 ⏰ Lunch, dinner

Port View (£–££)

Lively, late-night seafood spot set opposite the old Customs wharf. Choose your own fish from one of the live tanks.

✉ Jalan Haji Saman ☎ (088) 221753

Shiraz (££)

Kota Kinabalu's top Indian restaurant, which specialises in Moghul curries and *biryanis*.

✉ Lot 5, Block B, Sedco Kompleks, Jalan Sapuloh ☎ (088) 225088 ⏰ Lunch, dinner

Sri Kapitol (£–££)

Good Malay and Western specialities in this pleasant coffee shop.

✉ Hotel Capital, 23 Jalan Haji Saman ☎ (088) 231999 ⏰ Breakfast, lunch, dinner

Sri Melaka (£)

Excellent value restaurant with delicious Malay and Peranakan food.

✉ 9 Jalan Laiman Diki, Kampung Ayer ☎ (088) 55136 ⏰ Breakfast, lunch, dinner

Tanjung Aru Hawker Centre (£)

A range of hawker stalls set up along the city beach, serving mostly seafood dishes and traditional Malay specialities.

✉ Tanjung Aru beach ⏰ Dinner

Wishbone Café (££)

Attractive coffee house in the lobby of Kota Kinabalu's oldest hotel. Malaysian and Western cuisine.

✉ Jesselton Hotel, 69 Jalan Gaya ☎ (088) 223333 ⏰ Breakfast, lunch, dinner

Kuching

Beijing Riverbank (££)

A Chinese restaurant upstairs, and the 24-hour Traveller's Corner café downstairs, both enjoying a superb location overlooking the waterfront.

✉ Kuching Waterfront (opposite Hilton Hotel) ☎ (082) 234126 ⏰ Lunch, dinner

City Tower (££)

Gourmet Chinese restaurant at the top of the Civic Centre tower, with superb views over the city. Cheaper meals and snacks are on offer here, but there are similarly good views in the neighbouring cafeteria.

✉ Civic Centre, Jalan Budaya ☎ (082) 234396 ⏰ Lunch, dinner

Dulit Coffee House (£–££)

Attractive terrace café serving Western-style and local dishes, including excellent kebabs and hamburgers.

✉ Telang Usan Hotel, Jalan Ban Hock ☎ (082) 415588
🕐 Breakfast, lunch, dinner

Green Vegetarian (£)

A very basic Indian restaurant, which serves southern Indian vegetarian curries.

✉ 16 Main Bazaar
🕐 Breakfast, lunch, dinner

Hani's Bistro (£–££)

Good value Asian and Western food in a relaxed bistro atmosphere.

✉ Jalan Chan Chin Ann
☎ (082) 245793 🕐 Lunch, dinner

Lok Thian (££)

Excellent Thai cuisine served on the ground floor, gourmet Chinese cuisine served upstairs.

✉ Jalan Pending ☎ (082) 331310 🕐 Lunch, dinner

Open Air Market (£)

Rather misleading name for a covered hawker centre, with stalls serving a wide range of Chinese and Malay dishes.

✉ Jalan Market 🕐 Lunch, dinner

San Francisco Grill (££)

Pleasant steak restaurant with live piano music performed during the evenings.

✉ 7 Jalan Ban Hock ☎ (082) 258050 🕐 Lunch, dinner

See Good (££)

This is the city's top Chinese seafood restaurant. Choose your own lobster, crab, squid, prawns and clams, and have them cooked to your particular taste.

✉ Wisma Si Kiong, Jalan Bukit Mata (behind MAS offices) ☎ (082) 232609
🕐 Lunch, dinner

Sri Sarawak (£££)

Gourmet Malay and European cuisine and seafood, in a restaurant which enjoys superb views over the river.

✉ Riverside Majestic Hotel, Jalan Tuanku Abdul Rahman ☎ (082) 247777 🕐 Lunch, dinner

Top Spot Food Court (£)

Attractively landscaped outdoor hawker centre set on the roof of a multi-storey car park.

✉ Jalan Bukit Mata (behind MAS offices) 🕐 Lunch, dinner

Sandakan

Ming (£££)

Gourmet Chinese restaurant specialising in Cantonese and Szechuan cuisine.

✉ Sandakan Renaissance Hotel, Jalan Utara ☎ (089) 213299 🕐 Lunch, dinner

Supreme Garden (£)

Chinese vegetarian restaurant. The meals are good value and absolutely delicious.

✉ Block 30, Bandar Ramai-Ramai, Jalan Leila ☎ (089) 213292 🕐 Lunch, dinner

Trig Hill (£)

A series of open-air seafood stalls which enjoy superb views across the Sandakan bay.

✉ Jalan Bukit Bendera
🕐 Dinner

Vegetarian Food

Vegetarians are reasonably well catered-for in most large Malaysian towns and cities, where specialist Indian (and occasionally Chinese) vegetarian restaurants can be found. Elsewhere, it is more difficult to avoid meat, although fish is always available as an alternative. The Malay for 'I eat only vegetables' is *saya hanya makan sayuran*.

Peninsular Malaysia

Prices
Prices are for a double room, excluding breakfast and VAT:

£   = under RM60
££ = RM60–160
£££ = over RM160

Story-teller's Bar
Kuala Lumpur's crumbling Coliseum Hotel is relic of the days of Somerset Maugham, who once frequented the bar. Although faded and a little the worse for wear, the bar is full of character, still patronised by a mixed and vociferous crowd of Chinese businessmen, journalists, local shop-owners and curious travellers.

Kuala Lumpur

Carcosa Seri Negara (£££)
Luxury hotel occupying two elegantly restored colonial mansions set in beautiful gardens, the former residence and guest-house of the British resident Sir Frank Swettenham. Suites only.
✉ **Persiaran Mahameru, Taman Tasik Perdana** ☎ **(03) 282 1888**

Chamtan (££)
Good-value air-conditioned rooms, each with telephone and private bath. Good location – close to Masjid Jame.
✉ **62 Jalan Masjid India**
☎ **(03) 293 0144**

Coliseum (£)
Old and faded but quiet, clean and good value, with a convenient, central location. Try the famous bar and restaurant, on the ground floor.
✉ **100 Jalan Tuanku Abdul Rahman** ☎ **(03) 292 6270**

Heritage (£££)
This historic hotel has recently been restored. It forms a part of Kuala Lumpur's magnificent Moorish-style railway station building.
✉ **Railway Station, Jalan Sultan Hishamuddin** ☎ **(03) 273 5588**

Istana (£££)
One of Kuala Lumpur's most impressive luxury hotels, with a full range of facilities, including a swimming pool, garden and tennis courts. Much favoured by visiting VIPs.
✉ **73 Jalan Raja Chulan**
☎ **(03) 241 9988**

Malaya (££)
Reasonably priced hotel in centre of Chinatown, with air-conditioned rooms and *en suite* bath. Good café on ground floor.
✉ **162-164 Jalan Hang Lekir**
☎ **(03) 232 7722**

Pudu Raya (££)
Situated above Kuala Lumpur's busy inter-city bus station. Not a particularly pretty hotel, but clean, air-conditioned rooms with private bath, and convenient for late or early bus travellers.
✉ **4th floor, Hentian Pudaraya, Jalan Pudu** ☎ **(03) 232 1000**

Shangri-La (£££)
Glamorous luxury hotel in the heart of the Golden Triangle, conveniently close to many shopping centres, bars, restaurants and businesses.
✉ **11 Jalan Sultan Ismail**
☎ **(03) 232 2388**

Starlight (£–££)
Budget hotel set in the heart of Chinatown. Some rooms have air-conditioning and private bath.
✉ **90–92 Jalan Hang Kasturi**
☎ **(03) 238 9811**

Swiss Inn (££)
Another good value Chinatown hotel, handy for the Jalan Petaling night market, and with a good coffee shop.
✉ **62 Jalan Sultan** ☎ **(03) 232 3333**

Vistana (££)
Modern luxury hotel with reasonable prices located near Putra World Trade Centre. All rooms have air-conditioning, TV, bathroom

and mini-bar. Restaurants, pool, travel agency and airport limo service.

✉ **9 Jalan Lumut (off Jalan Ipoh)** ☎ **(03) 442 8000**

Cameron Highlands

Bala's Holiday Chalets (£)

Accommodation here ranges from dormitory beds to comfortable chalets equipped with private baths. There are pleasant gardens with good views of the countryside.

✉ **Tanah Rata** ☎ **(05) 491 1660**

Ye Olde Smokehouse (£££)

Beautifully renovated, 'olde English'-style hotel with features such as low ceilings, open log fires and a rose garden. Established in 1937. Suites only.

✉ **Tanah Rata** ☎ **(05) 491 1215**

Ipoh

Casuarina (£££)

Large luxury hotel located only 10 minutes from the airport, with a swimming pool, spa, restaurants and disco. Good views from rooms.

✉ **18 Jalan Gopeng** ☎ **(05) 255 5555**

Majestic (££)

Grand colonial hotel built at the turn of the century, and recently restored to its former glory. The better rooms have private verandahs, polished wooden floors and rattan furniture.

✉ **Railway Station, Jalan Club** ☎ **(05) 255 5605**

Kota Bharu

Indah (£–££)

Good-value hotel with air-conditioned rooms,

restaurant and car park. Good, central location overlooking Padang and Istana.

✉ **Jalan Tengku Besar** ☎ **(09) 748 5081**

Perdana (£££)

The best hotel in town, equipped with luxury rooms, good restaurant, swimming pool, tennis court and car park. Convenient location close to museum and cultural centre.

✉ **Jalan Mahmud** ☎ **(09) 774 4000**

Melaka

Heeren House (££)

Beautifully converted warehouse set on the Melaka River, with polished wood floors and antique furniture.

✉ **1 Jalan Tun Tan Cheng Lok** ☎ **(06) 281 4241**

Majestic (£)

A rambling old colonial-style hotel that has certainly seen better days, but nevertheless still offers a taste of faded elegance – and at budget prices.

✉ **188 Jalan Bunga Raya** ☎ **(06) 282 2455**

Melaka Youth Hostel (£)

Good value hostel with dormitory beds and lockers and a large and comfortable common room.

✉ **Lot 341, Taman Melaka Raya** ☎ **(06) 282 7915**

Ramada Renaissance (£££)

Melaka's top luxury hotel, with roof-top swimming pool, tennis and squash courts, disco and several restaurants.

✉ **Jalan Bendahara** ☎ **(06) 284 8888**

Hotel Taxes

A 5 per cent tax is charged on all hotel bills in Malaysia, and in the more expensive hotels a further 10 per cent charge is added on top of the tax. Quoted rates for cheap hotels generally include tax, but top-end establishments often omit it, quoting a price of, say, RM150++ ('plus-plus'). This means that the true rate is RM150 plus 5 per cent tax, plus 10 per cent service charge.

Malaysian Place-names

air terjun: waterfall; *bahru*: new; *bandar*: town; *batu*: rock; *bukit*: hill; *gua*: cave; *gunung*: mountain; *istana*: palace; *jalan*: road; *jambatan*: bridge; *kampung*: village; *kota*: fort; *kuala*: confluence or estuary; *lama*: old (as in 'former'); *leboh*: street; *lorong*: lane; *masjid*: mosque; *pasar*: market; *pulau*: island; *sungai*: river; *taman*: park; *tanjung*: point, headland; *tasik*: lake; *teluk*: bay.

Pulau Langkawi
Beach Garden (££)

Good value German-run beach hotel with swimming pool. Air-conditioning and private baths.

✉ **Pantai Cenang** ☎ **(04) 955 1363**

Pelangi Beach Resort (£££)

One of the island's most luxurious resorts, with Malay-style low-rise buildings spread throughout landscaped gardens.

✉ **Pantai Cenang** ☎ **(04) 955 1001**

Pulau Pangkor
Pangkor Laut Resort (£££)

Exclusive resort on private island off Pangkor's west coast. Luxury villas with pool, tennis courts, night-club and beautiful beaches.

✉ **Pulau Pangkor Laut** ☎ **(05) 699 1100**

Sea View (££)

Friendly hotel on beach, with outdoor restaurant and bar. Air-conditioned rooms and chalets with private bath.

✉ **Jalan Pasir Bogak, Pulau Pangkor** ☎ **(05) 685 1605**

Pulau Pinang
Baba's Guest House (£)

Friendly, family-run guest-house offering dormitory beds and air-conditioned rooms with private bath.

✉ **Batu Feringgi** ☎ **(04) 881 1686**

Bellevue (££)

Charming and historic hotel on top of Pinang Hill, with lovely gardens and superb views, especially at sunset. Five minutes' walk from top of funicular railway.

✉ **Bukit Bendera** ☎ **(04) 829 9500**

Continental (££)

Moderately priced hotel set in a good location near the main tourist sights. Room service, air-conditioning and private bath. The top floor restaurant has excellent views.

✉ **5 Jalan Pinang, George-town** ☎ **(04) 263 6388**

Eastern and Oriental (££–£££)

Built on the waterfront in 1885 by the same people who opened Raffles in Singapore, the E&O is one of the grand old hotels of the Orient.

✉ **10 Lebuh Farquhar, George-town** ☎ **(04) 263 0630**

Rasa Sayang (£££)

Pinang's top beach hotel has luxurious rooms, good restaurants and lots of character. Excellent pool surrounded by landscaped gardens.

✉ **Batu Feringgi** ☎ **(04) 881 1811**

Pulau Tioman
Berjaya Imperial Beach Resort (£££)

Well-run luxury resort, with air-conditioned chalets set in hillside gardens above one of Tioman's most beautiful beaches. Facilities include watersports, golf, tennis and horse-riding.

✉ **Pulau Tioman** ☎ **(09) 414 5445**

Nazri's Place (£–££)

Long-established backpackers' hang-out, with range of hut and chalet accommodation. Excellent restaurant overlooking beautiful beach.

✉ **Kampung Air Batang, Pulau Tioman** ☎ **No telephone**

East Malaysia

Kota Kinabalu

Backpackers Lodge (£)
Comfortable dormitory beds designed for the budget traveller, with shared bathroom, common room and laundry facilities.
✉ **25 Lorong Dewan, Australia Place** ☎ **(088) 261495**

Jesselton (£££)
Kota Kinabalu's oldest hotel, which was founded in 1954, has now been fully renovated to provide all modern facilities, but still exudes colonial charm and elegance.
✉ **69 Jalan Gaya** ☎ **(088) 223333**

Seaside Travellers Inn (£–££)
Budget family hotel in attractive beach house about 20km south of Kota Kinabalu. Tennis court, swimming pool, restaurant and barbecue.
✉ **1C Lorong Muntahan, Jalan Penampang** ☎ **(088) 750555**

Tanjung Aru Resort (£££)
Sabah's top luxury beach resort, run by Shangri-La. Attractive, landscaped gardens have been laid out beside a beautiful palm-fringed beach. Swimming pools, tennis courts, nine-hole pitch-and-putt, watersports, sailing, scuba-diving.
✉ **Tanjung Aru** ☎ **(088) 225800**

Kuching

Borneo (££)
Kuching's longest established hotel, with large, attractive rooms and attentive service.
✉ **30 Jalan Tabuan** ☎ **(082) 244122**

Kuching Hilton (£££)
Luxury hotel overlooking the waterfront. Its sister hotel, the Hilton Batang Ai Longhouse Resort, is situated on the lakeside, 275km east of Kuching, and offers jungle treks and longhouse visits.
✉ **Jalan Tuanku Abdul Rahman** ☎ **(082) 248200**

Telang Usan (££)
Friendly hotel run by Orang Ulu ('upriver people'), decorated with traditional art and crafts produced by the Kenyah natives of the interior.
✉ **Jalan Ban Hock** ☎ **(082) 415588**

Kundasang

Perkasa (££)
Luxury hotel near Mount Kinabalu, with superb panoramic views of the mountain. Facilities include room service, tennis court, restaurant and cocktail bar, and transport to national park is provided.
✉ **Kundasang, Sabah** ☎ **(088) 214142**

Sandakan

London (£)
Clean and efficient budget hotel offering modest air-conditioned rooms with private bath; in central location.
✉ **Block 10, Jalan Empat** ☎ **(089) 216371**

Ramada Renaissance (£££)
International luxury hotel, located close to the rain forest on the edge of town. Tennis and squash courts, fitness centre, golf course, disco.
✉ **Km 1, Jalan Utara** ☎ **(089) 213299**

Desert Islands

Travellers who really want to get away from it all can find solitude on the beaches of Pulau Tioman and the other islands of Malaysia's east coast. Most of the accommodation here is in the form of very basic beach huts or chalets, with no phones, no air-conditioning, and occasionally no electricity. You live on the beach, eat at a little seaside restaurant, and retire to your hut only to sleep.

Handicrafts &
Antiques

Batik and **Songket**
Malaysia is famous for the beautiful fabrics known as *batik* and *songket*. *Batik*, originally from Java, is made by painting patterns on cotton or silk using liquid wax, and dyeing the cloth several times to build up attractive designs. *Songket* is a delicate and expensive brocade made by interweaving coloured silk with threads of silver and gold.

Peninsular Malaysia

Kuala Lumpur

Batek Malaysia Berhad
Traditional handicrafts; branches all over Malaysia.
✉ **114 Jalan Bukit Bintang (Golden Triangle); Wisma Kraftangan, Jalan Tun Perak (near Masjid Jamek)** ☎ **(03) 986 1515**

Infokraf
A showcase for Malaysian handicrafts, including hand-painted *batik* fabric and *mengkuang* carpets.
✉ **26 Jalan Sultan Hishamuddin** ☎ **(03) 293 4929**

Karyaneka
Wide range of crafts, including *batik*, *songket*, embroidery, beads, carving, pottery, basketry, tapestry, pewter, brass and silver. Accepts major credit cards.
✉ **Kompleks Budaya Kraf, Jalan Conlay** ☎ **(03) 264 4344**

Royal Selangor Pewter
The company, which gives guided tours of the factory, produces pewter artefacts, from vases and bowls to tankards and chess sets.
✉ **231 Jalan Tuanku Abdul Rahman, Kuala Lumpur** ☎ **(03) 298 6244**

Ayer Hitam

Aw Pottery
Established over 100 years ago by a Chinese potter, this factory continues to produce hand-made pottery using a foot-powered wheel. The colourful glazed ware is sold at stalls lining the road at the Ayer Hitam crossroads, off the North–South Highway.
✉ **Ayer Hitam (87km north of Johor Bahru)**

Kota Bharu

Kampung Kraftangan
A 'handicraft village' where you can shop for silverware, *songket, batik* and wood-carving. Includes a museum and gallery, and has daily cultural shows.
✉ **Off Padang Merdeka (next to Istana Balai Besar)**

Wisma Songket
One of many *songket* and *batik* factories that line the road from Kota Bharu to Pantai Cinta Berahi. Kite-making workshop near by.
✉ **Kampung Penambang (2km north of city centre)**

Kuala Terengganu

Suterasemai Silk Centre
Silk factory where visitors can see the whole production process from the planting of mulberry trees to feed the silkworms, through the culture and harvesting of silkworm cocoons, to the finished fabric.
✉ **Kuala Ibai (6km south of Kuala Terengganu)**

Teratai
Restored shophouse in the middle of Chinatown, with pricey, high-quality hand-made arts and crafts.
✉ **Jalan Bandar**

Melaka

Jonkers Street
Also known as Jalan Hang Jebat, this Chinatown street has long been the centre of Melaka's famous antiques trade. The street is lined with fascinating antique shops, but its popularity means that prices may be higher than in neighbouring streets. Shop around!
✉ **Jalan Hang Jebat, Chinatown**

Karyaneka
Same chain as the shop in Kuala Lumpur (➤ 104), including the same fine range of goods. Accepts all major credit cards.
✉ **Jalan Kota** ☎ **(06) 281 3824**

Orang-Utan House
Bright and lively shop run by young locals, selling handicrafts, souvenirs, hand-painted T-shirts, etc. Very good value.
✉ **59 Lorong Hang Jebat, Chinatown**

Royal Selangor Pewter
The company, which produces artefacts to over 1,000 designs, has outlets all over the country.
✉ **Ground floor, Makhota Parade, Jalan Taman Merdeka** ☎ **(06) 282 2386**

Pulau Langkawi
Kompleks Budaya Kraf
Handicrafts centre which encompasses a craft museum and cultural theatre, plus outlets for Royal Selangor Pewter, Karyaneka, Batek Malaysia Berhad and other crafts shops.
✉ **Block B, Teluk Yu, Mukim Bohor (15 minutes' drive from the airport)** ☎ **(04) 959 1913**

Pulau Pinang
Asia Handicrafts
Small showroom with reasonable selection of *batik*, pewter, wood-carving and pottery.
✉ **Batu Feringgi** ☎ **(04) 881 1343**

Batek Malaysia Berhad
Range of traditional handicrafts, sold here and at branches all around the country.
✉ **Second floor, Kompleks Tuanku Abdul Razak (Komtar), Jalan Pinang, Georgetown** ☎ **(04) 262 1607**

Hong Giap Hang
Atmospheric old Chinese shophouse whose recesses are stacked with antiques and traditional furniture.
✉ **Jalan Pinang (opposite Police HQ)**

Royal Selangor Pewter
Another outlet of the pewter company.
✉ **Eastern and Oriental Hotel Arcade, 10 Lebuh Farquhar, Georgetown** ☎ **(04) 263 6742**

Yee Hoe Rattan
Selection of furniture and household items, ingeniously manufactured from bamboo and cane.
✉ **Lebuh Chulia**

East Malaysia

Kuching
Cahaya
Excellent range of handicrafts and souvenirs, including tribal artefacts such as carved wooden hornbills and ritual masks.
✉ **274 Jalan Datu Wee Kheng Chiang** ☎ **(082) 232218**

Fabriko
Attractively restored Chinese shophouse selling souvenirs and fashion on the ground floor, with a gallery-showroom of local handicrafts and antiques upstairs.
✉ **20 Main Bazaar**

Jalan Carpenter
This street, the main axis of Kuching's Chinatown, is lined at its western end with dozens of goldsmiths' shops (*kedai emas*).
✉ **Jalan Carpenter**

Sarakraf
Interesting shop piled high with handicrafts, including artefacts produced by Sarawak tribespeople. Run by the Sarawak Economic Development Corporation.
✉ **39 Main Bazaar** ☎ **(082) 258771**

The *Kris*
The *kris* is the traditional Malaysian dagger, with a distinctive wavy blade and an ornately decorated pistol-grip hilt. It has long been a symbol of honour, and was presented to young men to mark the passage from youth to manhood. The iron blade always has an odd number of waves, and the hilt, made of wood or ivory, is usually carved in the design of a bird's head.

Markets

Night Markets

The *pasar malam*, or 'night market', is a Malaysian institution found in towns and cities all over the country. Generally beginning around dusk and continuing into the small hours, it combines the functions of shopping, eating and entertainment, with music from Chinese, Malay and Filipino rock bands, and mouth-watering meals rustled up by the numerous hawker stalls.

Peninsular Malaysia

Kuala Lumpur
Central Market

This 1930s Art Deco building once housed the city's wet market, but is now given over to dozens of stalls and shops selling souvenirs, clothes, hats, bags, basketry, rattan, *batik*, kites and all kinds of other handicrafts. Also houses the Kuala Lumpur Handicraft Centre.

✉ **Jalan Hang Kasturi**
☎ **(03) 274 6542** ⏰ **Daily 9AM–10PM**

Chow Kit

KL's largest street market, where local people swarm along the board-walks and alleys looking for cheap clothes and shoes, fresh meat, fish, fruit and vegetables, books and magazines, music cassettes and CDs, and much more. Beware of pickpockets in this area.

✉ **Jalan Haji Hussein (off Jalan Tuanku Abdul Rahman)**
⏰ **Daily 9–5**

Jalan Petaling

The main axis of Kuala Lumpur's Chinatown is a busy crush of street-stalls and barrows selling all conceivable kinds of wares, from fresh vegetables to fake watches.

✉ **Jalan Petaling** ⏰ **Daily 9AM–10PM**

Pasar Malam (night market)

On Saturday nights the length of Jalan TAR is transformed into a bright and noisy night market, with musicians entertaining the crowds thronging among stalls that are piled high with cheap clothes, food and drink.

✉ **Jalan Tuanku Abdul Rahman** ⏰ **Sat 7PM–2AM**

Pasar Minggu (Sunday market)

Kuala Lumpur's 'Sunday market' actually begins on Saturday night – usually at around 6PM – and runs into the early hours of Sunday. This crowded maze of narrow alleys contains a number of interesting stalls selling handicrafts and textiles.

✉ **Jalan Raja Muda Musa, Kampung Bharu** ⏰ **Sat 6PM–2AM**

Pudu Market

This is one of the city's biggest and busiest wet markets, where you can make your choice from a mind-boggling variety of tropical fruits and vegetables, fresh seafood and anything from a deep-fried duck's foot to a side of pork. Make sure you bring your camera.

✉ **Jalan Pasar Baru (2km southeast of city centre)** ⏰ **Mon–Sat 8–4**

Kota Bharu
Central Market

Housed in an ugly, octagonal concrete building, and spilling into the surrounding streets, this is one of the most colourful markets in Malaysia. It's particularly enlivened by the local women in brightly coloured head-dresses, energetically touting for business beside their carefully arranged mountains of fruit and vegetables.

✉ **Jalan Hulu** ⏰ **Daily 9–5**

Kuala Terengganu
Pasar Besar Kedai Payang (Central Market)

A modern, multi-storey building overlooking the waterfront houses a lively market, which is well worth a look. There's a wet market on the ground floor, while the stalls on the upper floors include several good crafts shops selling *batik*, *songket* and brassware.

✉ **Jalan Bandar** 🕐 **Daily 8AM–9PM**

Melaka
Souvenir Market

A small collection of souvenir stalls lines a lane that leads from near A Famosa down to Glutton's Corner, but the quality of goods on sale here is generally rather poor. A better option would be to save your money for the antique shops in Jalan Hang Jebat – Chinatown (▶ 104).

✉ **Between Jalan Kota and Jalan Taman Merdeka** 🕐 **Daily 9–9**

Pulau Pinang
Batu Feringgi

The main street in Batu Feringgi comes alive in the evenings with market stalls selling souvenirs, *batik*, jewellery, T-shirts and snacks.

✉ **Batu Feringgi** 🕐 **Daily 6PM–1AM**

Rope Walk

This narrow street is lined with ancient junk shops, all stacked with a bewildering variety of antiques, chinaware, coins, clocks, lamps, glassware and other bric-a-brac.

✉ **Jalan Pintal Tali (off Lebuh Campbell)** 🕐 **Daily 9–6**

East Malaysia
Kota Kinabalu
Filipino Market

A two-storey building on the waterfront houses a lively market run mainly by Filipino immigrants. Stalls aimed at tourists sell hand-made baskets, sea-shells, souvenirs and tribal artefacts from Sabah.

✉ **Jalan Tun Fuad Stephens** 🕐 **Daily 8AM–9PM**

Jalan Gaya

On Sunday mornings Jalan Gaya comes alive with a bustle of market stalls selling all manner of goods, ranging from fruit, flowers and vegetables to pets, souvenirs and handicrafts.

✉ **Jalan Gaya** 🕐 **Sun 7–1**

Kuching
Pasar Minggu (Sunday market)

A colourful weekly bazaar where Bidayuh tribeswomen gather to sell their farm vegetables, along with produce such as wild honey, smoked turtle meat, wild boar, orchid plants and jungle fruit. There are good handicrafts stalls here, too, and excellent hawker food. The market is at its liveliest on Saturday night and early Sunday morning.

✉ **Jalan Satok, at junction with Jalan Palm (1km southwest of city centre)** 🕐 **Sat 2PM–Sun noon**

Wet Market

The waterfront of the west end of Jalan Gambier is lined with crowded stalls selling fresh fish, meat, fruit and vegetables.

✉ **Jalan Gambier** 🕐 **Daily 9AM–6PM**

Haggling

Bargaining is the norm when buying souvenirs in street markets. If you find something you want to buy, begin by offering around half the asking price, and then haggle in the hope of settling on an acceptable figure. Smile and keep the proceedings good-natured, and never make a firm offer unless you truly intend to buy.

Shopping Centres

Shopping in Comfort
Malaysia's countless modern shopping malls provide a comfortable, air-conditioned shopping environment. Although there are bargains to be had, KL cannot compete with Singapore when it comes to really low prices for cameras and electronic equipment. The best deals will be found on sports gear, watches, jewellery, music cassettes and Malaysian handicrafts. Most shopping centres open daily 10AM–10PM.

Peninsular Malaysia

Kuala Lumpur
Imbi Plaza
A small shopping centre on the southern edge of the Golden Triangle that specialises in a range of high-quality computers and computer accessories. The plaza offers a mind-boggling variety of low-cost software and CD-ROMs.
✉ Jalan Imbi

Kota Raya Plaza
This garish pink complex dominates the heart of Chinatown, and has an impressive range of quality outlets selling clothes, shoes, photographic equipment, music cassettes and CDs.
✉ Jalan Cheng Lock

Star Hill Shopping Centre
CK Tang's department store is the anchor for this collection of designer boutiques housed in airy colonnades around a curved atrium. Famous names whose clothes are featured here include Anne Klein, Bally, Ferragamo, Dunhill, Cerruti 1881 and Dolce e Gabbano.
✉ Jalan Bukit Bintang

Sungei Wang Plaza
The name means 'Money River', and cash aplenty flows through the tills of one of Kuala Lumpur's biggest shopping malls. Together with the neighbouring Bukit Bintang Plaza, it's built around the Metrojaya and Parkson-Grand superstores, and is strong on bargain electrical and electronic goods, sports gear, photographic equipment, clothes and shoes. There is also a vast selection of sweet and candy stalls, and a (very expensive) branch of Marks and Spencer.
✉ Jalan Sultan Ismail and Jalan Bukit Bintang

The Mall
This is the place to take the children. The Japanese-owned Yaohan department store is complemented by a fun park, complete with dodgems and carousels, a video arcade and virtual reality games.
✉ 100 Jalan Putra

The Weld
An up-market mall with expensive shops. The Chinese and Western fast-food restaurants and Delifrance café in the atrium make it a popular lunch spot for local office workers. The Times bookshop on the first floor has a good range of books about local history and nature, as well as English-language newspapers and magazines.
✉ 76 Jalan Raja Culan

Johor Bahru
Plaza Kota Raya
This huge pink, cream and peppermint green structure soars above the crumbling shophouses and colonial bungalows of central Johor Bahru, housing five levels of shops and restaurants, including a Co-op supermarket and several Western-style fast-food outlets. It will be joined some time in the future by others as part of an ongoing plan to re-develop the entire city centre.
✉ Jalan Trus

Melaka
Makhota Parade
A vast new shopping mall built on reclaimed land on Melaka's waterfront. Basement supermarket plus three levels of shops, covering just about everything you could think of: furniture, electronics, photographic, jewellery, sports, toys, and even a Suzuki car showroom. Food Court and fast-food restaurants, and top-floor video arcade and roller disco. MPH bookshop on ground floor.

✉ **Jalan Taman Merdeka**

Pulau Pinang
Komtar
Short for 'Kompleks Tuanku Adbul Razak', the Komtar's 65-storey tower is a prominent local landmark. The centre houses a labyrinth of shops, restaurants, cafés and amusement arcades, and two large department stores. There is also a small Times bookshop on the second level of the Yaohan department store. The shopping centre is conveniently located at the end of Jalan Pinang, a busy shopping street, and close to the antique and rattan goods shops of old Chinatown.

✉ **Jalan Pinang, Georgetown**

East Malaysia

Kota Kinabalu
Centre Point
Based on the Yaohan department store, this is the biggest of Kota Kinabalu's many shopping centres. There are a few good handicraft stores – look for Borneo Handicraft and Ceramic Shop on the ground floor in particular – and a bookshop on the second floor of Yaohan.

✉ **Jalan Pasar Baru**

Wisma Merdeka
A low-rise labyrinth of shops and fast-food restaurants at the northern end of the city centre. Borneo Craft on the first floor has a good selection of handicrafts as well as some fascinating books about Sabah's natural history and indigenous peoples.

✉ **Jalan Haji Salan and Jalan Lima Belas**

Kuching
Riverside Complex
A pleasant, air-conditioned plaza across the way from the Holiday Inn, with a supermarket, a department store and, on the first floor, a Times bookshop, which is the place to browse through an excellent range of English-language books. The mall lies at the east end of Kuching's attractive waterfront, not far from Main Bazaar and Jalan Carpenter.

✉ **Jalan Tuanku Abdul Rahman**

Sarawak Plaza
This sprawling mall stretches east from the Holiday Inn and contains several western fast-food outlets, including McDonald's, Pizza Hut and Kentucky Fried Chicken, as well as a range of interesting shops. A good selection of books on Sarawak can be found at Mohamed Yahia, in the basement, and the Rutu Colour Laboratory will process your holiday prints and slides overnight.

✉ **Jalan Abell**

Kites
Kite-flying was introduced to Malaysia from China, and has been a traditional pastime since the days of the 15th-century Melaka sultanate. Kites are still manufactured in Kelantan, and are popular as souvenirs. They are made of brightly coloured paper stretched over bamboo frames in the shape of birds, fish, cats or the moon.

Children's Attractions

Orang-Utans

The orang-utan sanctuaries at Sepilok, Sabah (► 78) and Semenggoh, Sarawak (► 90) give children the magical experience of being able to see these remarkable creatures at close quarters, when the young apes get their daily meal of bananas at special feeding platforms in the jungle. Remember that the orang-utans of Sepilok and Semenggoh are wild animals, and no matter how cute they look they can be aggressive, throwing dung and sticks at anyone who gets too close. They are very curious, however, and seem to be attracted by brightly coloured objects. A group of young apes at Sepilok once became so enamoured of one unfortunate tourist's clothes that they stripped him naked!

Peninsular Malaysia

Kuala Lumpur

Butterfly Farm

Get a close-up view of spectacular butterflies – such as the huge Rajah Brooke's Birdwing – and feel your skin crawl as you examine the tanks containing giant millipedes, scorpions and stick insects.

✉ Jalan Cenderasari ☎ (03) 293 4799 ⊙ Daily 9–5 (6 weekends and hols)

Sunway Lagoon

This is a particularly popular water-based theme park equipped with a wave pool, a paddling pool, water rides, and a 'Wild West' theme area.

✉ Bandar Sunway, Petaling Jaya ☎ (03) 735 6000 ⊙ Noon–9; 10AM–10:30PM weekends and public hols. Closed Tue 🍴 Fast food restaurants 💰 Expensive

Menara KL (KL Tower)

This telecommunications tower sits atop Bukit Nanas (Pineapple Hill) overlooking the Golden Triangle (► 35), and is a distinctive landmark on the city skyline. At 421m it is the third highest in the world, and the viewing galleries at the top provide a magnificent panorama of the city.

✉ Jalan Puncak (off Jalan P Ramlee) ☎ (03) 208 5448 ⊙ Daily 10–8 🍴 Seri Angkasa restaurant (£££) 💰 Moderate

Mines Wonderland

Theme park set in beautifully landscaped remains of open-cast tin mine. Range of white-knuckle rides plus Snow House, Animal Kingdom, Musical Fountain and nightly laser show.

✉ Jalan Sungai Besi ☎ (03) 942 5010 ⊙ Daily 4PM–11PM 🍴 Restaurant and snack bars (££) 💰 Expensive

Zoo Negara

► 69.

In addition to the animal enclosures, there are daily animal shows featuring orang-utans, sea-lions and birds, and kids can enjoy rides on an elephant, camel or donkey. The aquarium and the insect and reptile houses are particularly fascinating for youngsters.

✉ Ulu Kelang, 13km north-east of Kuala Lumpur ☎ (03) 408 3422 ⊙ Daily 9–5 💰 Moderate

Internet cafés

The Malaysian capital is well served by cafés where you can enjoy a coffee while junior surfs the net. The following are popular:

Global Café

✉ FIII, The Bangsar, Bukit Bandaraya ☎ (03) 284 4717 (e-mail: info@globalcafe.com.my) ⊙ Daily 8–8

Global Village Cybercafé

✉ 193A, Jalan 552/24, Petaling Jaya ☎ (03) 773 0618 (e-mail: info@gv.net.my) ⊙ Daily 8–8

Melaka

Crocodile Farm

Malaysia's largest crocodile farm rears over 100 varieties of crocodile, including albinos. Feeding time is always the most popular part of the day.

✉ Ayer Keroh (► 40) ⊙ Daily 9–6 💰 Cheap

Makhota Parade

This vast new shopping centre (► 108) may not be an obvious choice, but it has several attractions ideal for the older children, including a video games arcade and a roller-disco.

✉ Jalan Taman Merdeka
🕐 Daily 10–10

Melaka Zoo and Ayer Keroh Lake

Melaka's zoo is small but prettily landscaped, with a good selection of Malaysian wildlife. The nearby lake has paddle-boats and canoes for hire.

✉ Ayer Keroh (► 40)
🕐 Daily 9–6 💰 Cheap

Pulau Pinang
Bukit Bendera
(► 62)

A trip on the funicular railway to the summit of Pinang Hill makes an interesting excursion for everyone. There is also the added attraction of a playground at the top, as well as hiking trails, bird-watching and a tea-room.

✉ Ayer Itam, 6km west of George Town 🕐 Trains run daily every 30 mins, 6:30AM–9:30PM 💰 Cheap

Butterfly Farm
(► 62)

Children can get a close-up view of not only colourful butterflies but also a range of creatures including tropical insects like spiders, giant millipedes and scorpions. The park also has a variety of species of frogs and reptiles, including the iguana-like 'oriental water dragon'.

✉ Teluk Bahang ☎ (04) 885 1253 🕐 Daily 9–5 (6PM weekends and hols) 💰 Cheap

East Malaysia

Beaches

Children love the beach, and there are several excellent ones to visit in East Malaysia. The area's best family beaches include Damai Beach at Santubong, near Kuching, Sarawak (► 84) and Tanjung Aru, a few kilometres to the south of Kota Kinabalu, Sabah (► 74).

Caves

Older children are bound to enjoy the adventure of exploring the impressive caves at Niah (► 88), Gunung Mulu, notably the Deer Cave and Clearwater Cave (► 88) and Gomantong (► 76), and learning about the wildlife that inhabits these huge limestone caverns.

Trains

The train journey from Beaufort to Tenom, southwest of Kota Kinabalu, follows a scenic route through the gorge of the Padas River (► 76). You can make the trip on the tiny railcar (comfortably air-conditioned, with just 13 seats) in an hour and a half, or in two hours on a diesel-hauled train. To make sure you get the best views, sit on the right-hand side (heading from Beaufort to Tenom).

✉ Booking Office: Tanjung Aru Station, Kota Kinabalu
☎ (088) 254611 🕐 Four trains daily, departing Beaufort 8:25AM, 10:50AM, 1:55PM and 3:50PM Mon–Sat; 6:45AM, 10:50AM, 2:30PM and 4:05PM Sun 🚌 Minibus from Kota Kinabalu 💰 Moderate

The Heat Factor

Don't forget that young ones are especially vulnerable to the effects of the tropical sun. Take along plenty of sun-screen, see that they wear sun hats or baseball caps and are well covered during the middle of the day, and make sure that they drink plenty of fluids to avoid dehydration. Nothing is more certain to spoil a holiday than a bad case of sunburn.

Cultural Shows

Let's Dance
The most popular of Malaysia's traditional dances is the *joget*, performed during cultural celebrations and Malay wedding ceremonies. Both men and women take part in the elaborate, fast-tempo dance, and although they weave in and out they never touch. The dance has Portuguese origins, and is better known in Melaka as the *cakuncak*.

Peninsular Malaysia

Kuala Lumpur
Central Market
Cultural performances are held every day in the outdoor auditorium, adjacent to the Central Market building.
⊠ **Jalan Hang Kasturi**
☎ **(03) 274 6542** Ⓒ **Evening**

Malaysian Tourist Information Complex
Performances of traditional Malay music and dance are held every day in the auditorium.
Ⓜ **109 Jalan Ampang** ☎ **(03) 264 3929** Ⓒ **Tue, Thu and Sat 3:30PM and 7.30PM**

Seri Melayu Restaurant
A combined Malay banquet and cultural show is the speciality here.
⊠ **Kompleks Budaya Kraf, Jalan Conlay** ☎ **(03) 245 1833**
Ⓒ **Dinner only**

Melaka
Medan Portugis
This 'village square' on the coast south of Melaka is at the heart of the town's Portuguese-Malay community. Diners at the restaurants here can enjoy a performance of live Portuguese and Malay music.
⊠ **Medan Portugis (3km east of city centre)** ☎ **(06) 284 8067**
Ⓒ **Sat only, 8PM**

Mini Malaysia
Cultural shows are performed daily at this heritage park at Ayer Keroh (► 40).
⊠ **Ayer Keroh (12km north of Melaka)** ☎ **(06) 232 3176**
Ⓒ **Daily 9–6**

Sound and Light Show
Performances are held at an open-air auditorium on the Padang near A Famosa. Coloured floodlights and a booming sound-track dramatise the story of Melaka's history.
⊠ **Jalan Kota** Ⓒ **Nightly 8PM (in Malay), 9:30PM (in English)**
Ⓜ **Moderate**

Pulau Pinang
Istana Theatre-Restaurant
A banquet of classic Malay cuisine is accompanied by a performance of traditional music and dance.
⊠ **Pinang Cultural Centre, Jalan Hassan Abbas, Teluk Bahang** ☎ **(04) 885 1175**
Ⓒ **Evening**

East Malaysia

Kota Kinabalu
During the month of May, the indigenous peoples celebrate the 'Pesta Kaamatan' (Harvest Festival). These colourful village ceremonies culminate in the state festival held in Penampang (13km south of Kota Kinabalu).
⊠ **Hongkod Koisaan, Penampang** Ⓒ **30 & 31 May**

Kuching
Sarawak Cultural Village
Demonstrations of traditional activities such as basket-weaving and blowpipe target-practice, plus displays of music, dance and costumes from the various tribal cultures of the Sarawak area.
⊠ **Kampung Budaya Sarawak, Pantai Damai, Santubong (40km north of Kuching)** ☎ **(082) 846411** Ⓒ **Daily 9–12:30, 2–5:30. Dance performances begin at 11:30 and 4:30**

Nightlife

Peninsular Malaysia

Kuala Lumpur
Club OZ

An up-market discothèque in the luxury Shangri-La Hotel in the Golden Triangle. Dance music, live bands, professional DJs and smart dress code.

✉ **Shangri-La Hotel, Jalan Sultan Ismail** ☎ **(03) 232 2388** ⊙ **Daily 9PM–2AM**

Hard Rock Café

One of the liveliest night-spots in Kuala Lumpur, offering live bands and dance music.

✉ **Concorde Hotel, 2 Jalan Sultan Ismail** ☎ **(03) 244 2200** ⊙ **Daily 9PM–2AM (3AM Fri and Sat). Live bands begin 11PM**

President Cinema

Screens a selection of Hollywood blockbusters (in English, with Malay subtitles) as well as the usual Bruce Lee/Jackie Chan-type action movies.

✉ **Sungai Wang Plaza, Jalan Sultan Ismail** ☎ **(03) 248 0084** ⊙ **Daily 11AM–11PM**

Sharks Club

'Fun pub' atmosphere, with bar games, good music, and an open-air barbecue. Live bands perform on weekends. Popular with ex-pats and tourists.

✉ **23 Jalan Sultan Ismail** ☎ **(03) 241 7878** ⊙ **Open 24 hours a day**

Melaka
Sparks

Disco and night-club – popular with a young crowd. Mixture of DJs and live bands.

✉ **Top floor, Makhota Parade, Jalan Taman Merdeka** ⊙ **Thu–Sat 8PM–2AM**

Pulau Pinang
20 Leith Street

Stylish and popular bar and bistro which has dance music played later in the evenings; set in beautifully renovated Chinese shophouse. A favourite hang-out for ex-pats and tourists.

✉ **20 Lebuh Leith, Georgetown** ☎ **(04) 261 8573** ⊙ **Daily 6PM–2AM (3AM Fri–Sat)**

East Malaysia

Kota Kinabalu
Rocky's Fun Pub

Lively bar and café in the middle of Kota Kinabalu's main city-centre street, with disco and karaoke nights, with a mixed clientele of locals, expatriates and tourists.

✉ **52 Jalan Gaya** ⊙ **Daily 6PM–2AM**

Kuching
Dai Ichi Karaoke and Lounge

Top-notch karaoke bar, with state-of-the-art sound system, popular with locals and tourists alike. When in Rome…

✉ **255–256 Jalan Tuanku Abdul Rahman** ☎ **(082) 233363** ⊙ **Daily 8:30PM–2AM (3AM weekends and public hols)**

Peppers

Kuching's most popular disco has a dance floor downstairs and karaoke lounge upstairs. Ladies' nights on Wednesday and Friday.

✉ **Kuching Hilton, Jalan Tuanku Abdul Rahman** ☎ **(082) 248200** ⊙ **Daily 8:30PM–2AM**

The Place to Be

KL's Golden Triangle has recently been superceded as the focus of the city's trendiest nightlife by the suburban centre of Bangsar, about 4km to the southwest. Formerly a quiet, middle-class residential area, Bangsar now offers dozens of excellent (if expensive) restaurants, and many stylish clubs and bars, frequented by young, professional Malaysians and the European and American expatriate communities.

Sports

Sporting Malaysians

The government is keen to promote Malaysia's sporting profile, and in addition to hosting the Commonwealth Games in 1998 it has instituted many annual international events like the Tour de Langkawi cycle race and the Kinabalu Climbathon. In 1997 it sponsored a mountaineering team that hopes to put the first Malaysian on the summit of Everest.

Malaysians are enthusiastic about sports, and particularly enjoy soccer, badminton, tennis, squash and cricket. They are also especially fond of outdoor activities, such as hiking, cycling and canoeing. Not surprisingly, there is no shortage of opportunities for the holiday-maker who wants to indulge in a little sporting activity.

Angling

Malaysia has excellent opportunities for angling, ranging from big-game fishing for black marlin in the waters of the South China Sea, to freshwater fishing in the lakes and rivers of the interior, where the famous *mahsa* (a relative of the Indian *mahseer*) is generally considered to be the most challenging prey. Special permits are required for anyone wanting to fish in national parks and marine parks.

Department of Fisheries, Malaysia ✉ **Eighth and ninth floors, Wisma Tani, Jalan Sultan Salahuddin, 50628 Kuala Lumpur** ☎ **(03) 298 2011**

Cave Exploring

Malaysia is one of the world's top sites for cave exploration. Sarawak offers some of the best caving experiences, in the vast chambers of the fascinating Mulu National Park and the Niah Caves, but there are also interesting caves at Gomantong in Sabah, and in various locations in Peninsular Malaysia. Beginners can arrange adventure caving trips through specialist tour operators in Kuching, Miri and Kuala Lumpur.

Borneo Overland Services ✉ **37 Rashawan Building, Brooke Road, PO Box 1509, 98008 Miri, Sarawak** ☎ **(085) 80255**

Golf

Golf is extremely popular in Malaysia. Some of the more outstanding courses include:

Kuala Lumpur
Royal Selangor Golf Club

Founded in 1893, this is the second oldest club in the country. It offers two challenging championship courses. Venue for the Malaysian Open.

✉ **PO Box 11051, 50734 Kuala Lumpur** ☎ **(03) 984 8433**

Saujana Golf and Country Club

The most expensive and prestigious club in Malaysia, the Saujana is one of the world's top 100 courses.

@ **PO Box 610, 46770 Petaling Jaya** ☎ **(03) 746 1466**

Cameron Highlands
Cameron Highlands Golf Club

This charming but difficult course is laid out in a beautiful setting among the jungle-clad hills. Founded as a five-hole course in 1935, it was extended to 18 holes in 1974.

✉ **15–16 Main Road, PO Box 25, 39007 Tanah Rata** ☎ **(05) 491 1154**

Kuching
Damai Beach Golf Course

An international-class golf course, designed by Arnold Palmer, in a dramatic and beautiful location between the peak of Gunung Santubong and the South China Sea.

✉ Jalan Santubong, PO Box 400, 93902 Kuching ☎ (082) 846088

Pulau Pinang
Bukit Jambul Country Club
Designed by Robert Trent Jones, this is one of Malaysia's most scenically impressive golf courses, meandering among rock outcrops and tropical fruit trees.
✉ 2 Jalan Bukit Jambul, 11900 Bayan Lepas, Pinang ☎ (04) 644 2255

Pulau Tioman
Tioman Island Golf Club
Set amid swaying palms, above the turquoise waters of the South China Sea, this 18-hole, par 71 course offers lucky members the opportunity of golfing in paradise. The clubhouse overlooks the beach as well as the 18th green. Part of the Berjaya Imperial Beach Resort.
✉ Pulau Tioman, PO Box 4, 86807 Mersing, Johor ☎ (09) 414 5445

Jungle Trekking
Malaysia offers a wide variety of hiking trails through some of the world's most beautiful primary rain forest, rich in exotic flora and fauna. Treks range from a one-hour stroll to multi-day expeditions. Marked trails are concentrated in national parks and forest reserves such as Taman Negara (➤ 26), Kinabalu (➤ 76), Gunung Mulu (➤ 88), Bako (➤ 87), Taman Alam Kuala Selangor (➤ 68) and Templer Park (➤ 69).
Association of Backpackers Malaysia ✉ 6 Jalan SS3/33,

47300 Petaling Jaya, Selangor ☎ (03) 775 6249

Scuba-diving
The crystal clear waters of the South China Sea provide some of the finest diving in the world, and spectacular dive sites such as Sipadan, on the southeast coast of Sabah, are world-famous. A number of diving operators offer courses of instruction for beginners, as well as complete back-up services for experienced divers.
Borneo Divers ✉ 4th floor, Wisma Sabah, 8800 Kota Kinabalu, Sabah ☎ (088) 222226

Watersports
There are plenty of facilities for dinghy sailing, windsurfing, water-skiing, canoeing and a number of other water-based activities to be found at many of Malaysia's more popular beach resorts, including Pulau Langkawi, Pulau Pangkor, Pulau Tioman, Pulau Pinang, Kampung Cerating, Desaru, Santubaong (Sarawak) and Tanjung Aru (Kota Kinabalu, Sabah).

White-water Rafting
This exhilarating sport is becoming more and more popular in Malaysia, and is now available at a number of popular sites, including the Padas River in Sabah, the Skrang River in, Sarawak and the Tembeling River in Pahang, in Peninsular Malaysia.
Borneo Memories ✉ Second floor, Block B, Asia City Complex, Kota Kinabalu ☎ (088) 255248

Trekking
Trekking in Malaysia's national parks provides the opportunity to experience one of the world's most diverse ecosystems. The country boasts over 8,000 species of flowering plants, 200 of mammals, 450 of birds, 250 of reptiles and 150,000 of insects (with many more yet to be discovered). The national flower is the hibiscus (known locally as *bunga raya*) and the national butterfly is the Rajah Brooke birdwing, whose large black wings are adorned with a flash of iridescent green.

What's On When

Pilgrimage of Pain

Thaipusam draws crowds of 100,000 pilgrims, devotees and on-lookers to the Batu Caves, where masochistic penitents pierce their tongues and cheeks with skewers, or suspend pots of milk from hooks embedded in their skin, and carry *kavadis* – large, cage-like structures, decorated with flowers, feathers and religious images, borne on long spikes which pierce the bearers' flesh.

The dates of religious festivals are based on the lunar calendar, and occur about 11 days earlier each year.

January

Thaipusam: Hindu festival when devotees pay homage to Lord Muruga. In Kuala Lumpur, there is a huge procession from the Sri Mahamariamman temple to Batu Caves (see panel)

February

Chinese New Year: two-week festival celebrated enthusiastically in KL and Pinang, with lantern decorations, huge fire-crackers and lion dances
Hari Raya Aidilfitri: Muslim festival celebrating the end of Ramadan, the month of fasting and abstinence, marked by a two-day national holiday
Le Tour de Langkawi: gruelling 13-day cycle race with legs in each of Malaysia's states, culminating in Langkawi

April

Easter: candle-lit processions from St Peter's Church in Melaka on Palm Sunday
Malaysian World Motorcycle Grand Prix: Shah Alam

May

Wesak Day: celebrates the Buddha's birth, enlightenment and achievement of Nirvana, marked by ceremonies at Buddhist temples (especially in Pinang and Melaka), including the release of caged birds (symbolising the release of captive souls)
Sabah International Triathlon: Kota Kinabalu

International Kite Festival: Kota Bharu
International Dragon Boat Festival: Pinang
Pinang International Triathlon: Batu Feringgi

June

Gawai Dyak: the end of the rice harvest is celebrated by Sarawak's Dyak people with singing, dancing, various blowpipe events and much drinking of tuak, a potent rice wine
Sabah Dragon Boat Race: Kota Kinabalu
Cultural Festival: Marang

August

Cultural Festival: Kuching
Cultural Festival: Pinang
Hari Kebengsaan: Malaysia's national day, marked with parades through Kuala Lumpur and cultural performances in the Lake Gardens

September

Mount Kinabalu International Climbathon: Kinabalu National Park
Lantern Festival: Georgetown Esplanade, Pinang
Beach Carnival: Pinang

October

Deepavali: Hindu 'Festival of Light', celebrating the return from exile of Lord Rama, marked by fire-walking ceremonies at Hindu temples. National holiday except in East Malaysia

December

Christmas: widely celebrated in Malaysia by Christians and non-Christians alike, with spectacular decorations set up in hotels and shopping centres

Practical
Matters

TIME DIFFERENCES

GMT
12 noon

Malaysia
8PM

Germany
1PM

USA (NY)
7AM

Netherlands
1PM

Spain
1PM

BEFORE YOU GO

WHAT YOU NEED

● Required
○ Suggested
▲ Not required

	UK	Germany	USA	Netherlands	Spain
Passport/National Identity Card	●	●	●	●	●
Visa	▲	▲	▲	▲	▲
Onward or Return Ticket	●	●	●	●	●
Health Inoculations (Hepatitis A and B, Cholera, Polio, Tetanus, Typhoid)	○	○	○	○	○
Health Documentation (► 123, Health)	○	○	○	○	○
Travel Insurance	○	○	○	○	○
Driving Licence (International)	●	●	●	●	●
Car Insurance Certificate (if own car)	●	●	●	●	●
Car Registration Document (if own car)	●	●	●	●	●

WHEN TO GO

Kuala Lumpur

▬▬▬ High season
▭▭▭ Low season

26°C	27°C	27°C	27°C	27°C	27°C	27°C	27°C	26°C	26°C	26°C	26°C
JAN	FEB	MAR	APR	MAY	JUN	JUL	AUG	SEP	OCT	NOV	DEC

Very wet   Wet   Sun   Sunshine & showers

TOURIST OFFICES

In the UK
Malaysia Tourism
Promotion Board
(Tourism Malaysia)
Malaysia House
57 Trafalgar Square
London WC2N 5DU
☎ 0171 930 7932
Fax: 0171 930 9015

In the USA
Malaysia Tourism
Promotion Board
(Tourism Malaysia)
595 Madison Avenue
Suite 1800
New York, NY 10022
☎ 212/754 1113/4/5/7
Fax: 212/754 1116

Malaysia Tourism
Promotion Board
(Tourism Malaysia)
818, Suite 804
West 7th Street
Los Angeles, CA 90017
☎ 213/689 9702
Fax: 213/689 1530

POLICE 999

AMBULANCE 999

FIRE 994

WHEN YOU ARE THERE

ARRIVING

Malaysia is served by more than 30 international airlines flying to Kuala Lumpur from all over the world. Malaysia Airlines, together with British Airways, are the country's major scheduled operators. The non-stop flight time from London is approximately 13 hours.

Kuala Lumpur (Subang) Airport

Kilometres to city centre	Journey times	
	🚆	N/A
24 kilometres	🚌	45 minutes
	🚗	30 minutes

Kuala Lumpur (Sapang) Airport
– due for completion early 1998

Kilometres to city centre	Journey times	
	🚆	35 minutes
70 kilometres	🚌	90 minutes
	🚗	60 minutes

MONEY

The unit of currency is the Malaysian *ringgit* (RM), though unofficially it is still called the Malaysian dollar. It is divided into 100 *sen*. Coins in circulation are 1, 5, 10, 20 and 50 *sen* and 1 *ringgit*; banknotes are 1, 2, 5, 10, 20, 50, 100, 500 and 1,000 *ringgit*. The best rates are available at the airports and from local money changers. Few hotels offer the current rate; shop around for the best deal. Travellers' cheques can be cashed at banks, money changers, hotels, large department stores and shopping complexes. Credit cards are widely accepted.

TIME

 Malaysia is eight hours ahead of Greenwich Mean Time (GMT+8) throughout the year.

CUSTOMS

 YES

Goods Obtained Duty Free (Limits for importation into Malaysia):
Alcohol: 1L
Cigarettes: 200 *or*
Cigars: 50 *or*
Tobacco: 225g
Souvenirs and gifts: not exceeding RM200
Amounts above these limits (plus carpets, garments, clothing accessories, jewellery, chocolates and handbags) are liable to duty. Visitors bringing in dutiable goods may have to pay a deposit for temporary importation (refundable on departure).
Items such as cameras, video equipment, portable radio cassette players, cameras, watches, pens, lighters, perfumes and cosmetics do not attract duty.

 NO

Drugs **(penalty: death),** weapons (including imitations), fire crackers, counterfeit currency, obscene material.

EMBASSIES AND HIGH COMMISSIONS

UK
(03) 2482122
(High Commission)

Germany
(03) 2429666
(Embassy)

USA
(03) 2489011
(Embassy)

Netherlands
(03) 2421341
(Embassy)

Spain
(03) 2484868
(Embassy)

WHEN YOU ARE THERE

TOURIST OFFICES

Malaysia Tourism Promotion Board (Tourism Malaysia)

Head Office
● 17th Floor
  Menara Dato Onn
  Putra Trade Centre
  45 Jalan Tun Ismail
  50480 Kuala Lumpur
  ☎ (03) 2935188

Northern Region
● 10 Jalan Tun Syed Sheh
  Barakbah
  10200 Penang
  ☎ (04) 2619067

Southern Region
● No 1, 4th Floor
  Tun Abdul Razak Complex
  Jalan Wong Ah Fook
  80000 Johor Bahru
  ☎ (07) 2223591

East Coast Region
● 2243, Ground Floor
  Wisma MCIS
  Jalan Sultan Zainal Abidin
  20000 Kuala Terengganu
  ☎ (09) 6221433

Sabah
● Ground Floor
  Bangunan EON CMG Life
  1 Jalan Sagunting
  88000 Kota Kinabalu
  ☎ (088) 248698

Sarawak
● 2nd Floor
  Bangunan Rugayah
  Jalan Song Thian Cheok
  93100 Kuching
  ☎ (082) 246575

NATIONAL HOLIDAYS

J	F	M	A	M	J	J	A	S	O	N	D
3	2		(2)	3	1	1	1		1	1	1

1 Jan	New Year's Day (except Johor, Kedah, Kelantan, Perlis, Terengganu)
Jan/Feb	Chinese New Year
Jan/Feb	Hari Raya Puasa
Apr	Hari Raya Haji
Apr/May	Awal Muharram (Muslim New Year)
1 May	Labour Day
May	Wesak Day
Jun (1st Sat)	The King's (Yang di-Pertuan Agong) Birthday
Jul	Birthday of the Prophet Muhammad
31 Aug	National Day
Oct/Nov	Deepvali (except Sarawak and Labuan)
25 Dec	Christmas Day

OPENING HOURS

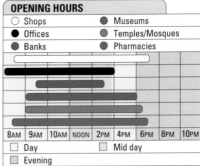

○ Shops   ● Museums
● Offices   ● Temples/Mosques
● Banks   ● Pharmacies

| 8AM | 9AM | 10AM | NOON | 2PM | 4PM | 6PM | 8PM | 10PM |

☐ Day   ☐ Mid day
☐ Evening

In addition to the times in the chart, supermarkets, department stores, shopping malls and Chinese Emporiums open 10AM to 10PM (some also open Sundays). In Kelantan, Terengganu, Perlis and Kedah, shops are closed Thursday afternoon and all day Friday, but open Sunday. Banks open weekdays as times in chart, they also open Saturday 9:30 to 11:30AM. In Kelantan, Terengganu, Perlis and Kedah, banks open 9:30 to 11:30AM Thursday and are closed Friday. Temples are closed to visitors during prayer times.

DRIVE ON THE
LEFT

TOILETS
CHARGE

PUBLIC TRANSPORT

Internal Flights Malaysia Airlines links Kuala Lumpur to all major cities and towns of the peninsula (an hour at most) and to East Malaysia (at least two hours). Other airlines, including Pelangi Air and Berjaya Air, service popular tourist destinations, including resort islands.

Trains Malayan Railways (KTM) provide a comfortable and economical service that extends from north to south and east to west in Peninsular Malaysia, with Kuala Lumpur as the hub. Express trains, stopping only at major towns, provide the best service for tourists.

Long Distance Buses There are regular bus services to most parts of the country. Express (air-conditioned) buses connecting all major towns are the most comfortable. Buses between, and within, states are not air-conditioned. Tickets are cheap but services do not always run on time.

Ferries No sea connection exists between the peninsula and East Malaysia, however, there are regular ferry services between the peninsula and its main offshore islands: Langkawi (from Kuala Perlis and Kuala Kedah), Penang (from Butterworth), Pangkor (from Lumut), and Tioman (from Mersing).

Urban Transport Kuala Lumpur is served by the fast KTM Komuter electric train which goes out to the suburbs, plus the modern LRT (Light Rail Transit) system which runs above ground through the city centre. There are also buses and minibuses. Transport elsewhere is by bus or rickshaw.

CAR RENTAL

Many of the international car-hire companies have desks at airports, large hotels and major shopping and office complexes. There are also numerous local operators. You can normally pick a car up in one city and drop it off in another. You will need an international driving licence. Cars all have air-conditioning.

TAXIS

Taxis can be hailed road-side, hired from a taxi stand, or booked by phone. Most have a meter; if it's not on, agree a price beforehand. There is a surcharge for trips between midnight and 6AM; more than two passengers; luggage; and phone bookings. For airport and railway station taxis, buy coupons at the taxi desk.

DRIVING

Speed limit on expressways and highways: **110kph**

Speed limit on trunk roads: **80kph**

Speed limit on urban roads: **50kph**

The wearing of seat belts is compulsory, though belts are fitted to front seats only.

There is random breath-testing. Limit: 0.08% blood/alcohol level.

Petrol is inexpensive. Unleaded petrol is available in most areas. There are frequent petrol stations, especially in or on the fringes of towns. They have toilet facilities and sell drinks (important to prevent dehydration). Many operate 24 hours a day and accept credit cards as payment.

If you break down in a hired car you should follow the instructions given in the documentation; most international rental firms provide a rescue service. The Automobile Association of Malaysia (AAM), 25 Jalan Yap Kwan Seng, Kuala Lumpur, ☎ (03) 2425777, will let you join its organisation with a letter of introduction from your own automobile association.

Ruler markings (CENTIMETRES 0–8, INCHES 0–3)

PERSONAL SAFETY

Malaysia is relatively safe – violent crimes against tourists are unknown. Pick-pocketing and bag snatching is a problem in some cities. If you need help, or lose an item of value, contact the Tourist Police (caps with chequered bands) who speak English. For safety:

- Carry only what you need in a safe place on your person.
- Leave valuables in your hotel deposit box.
- Do not take short cuts down deserted streets at night.
- Bathing – keep to patrolled hotel beaches.

Police assistance:
☎ **999** from any call box

TELEPHONES

Public telephones are coin or card operated. Coin phones can only be used to make calls within the country and require coins of 10, 20 and 50 *sen* and 1 *ringgit*. Card phones (*Kadfon*) can be used for local and international calls. Telekom cards are available from most retail outlets in values of 3, 5, 10, 20 and 50 *ringgit*.

International Dialling Codes

From Malaysia to:	
UK:	007 44
Germany:	007 49
USA:	007 1
Netherlands:	007 31
Spain:	007 34

POST

Post Offices
There are post offices in most cities and towns. The general post office: 2nd Floor, Dayabumi Complex, Jalan Sultan Hishamuddin, Kuala Lumpur, is open 8–6 (10–12:45 Sun). Other offices:
Open: 8–5 (noon Sat)
Closed: Sun (Fri: Kedah, Kelantan, Terengganu)
☎ (03) 274 1122 (KL)

ELECTRICITY

The power supply in Malaysia is: 220–240 volts Sockets accept three-square-pin (UK-style) plugs, although some older places have three-round-pin plugs. An adaptor is needed for continental appliances, and a voltage transformer for appliances operating on 100–120 volts.

TIPS/GRATUITIES

Yes ✓ No ✗		
Hotels (service included)	✗	
Restaurants (service included)	✗	
Cafés (service included)	✗	
Taxis	✗	
Rickshaws	✗	
Tour guides	✓	10%
Porters	✓	RM2–5
Chambermaids	✓	RM2–5
Hairdressers	✗	
Toilets	✓	change

PHOTOGRAPHY

Best times to photograph: Malaysia has a lot of natural colour, to capture it at its best take photographs early in the morning or late in the afternoon.
Where to buy film: film is cheap and readily available in Malaysia, but best bought in cities rather than in the countryside where proper storage conditions cannot be guaranteed.
Restrictions: there is usually no objection to taking photographs in places of worship (temples and mosques), but always ask first.

HEALTH

Insurance
Malaysia does not have reciprocal health service agreements with other countries so it is essential you take out medical insurance. Medical treatment is available at government hospitals, specialist centres and private clinics in most towns.

Dental Services
Dental treatment has to be paid for but private medical insurance will cover costs. If you have to pay for treatment make sure you keep all documentation to claim it back later.

Sun Advice
With temperatures that fluctuate little throughout the year (an average of between 21 and 32°C) you can get sunburnt at any time. The tropical sun is deceptively strong. Wear a shady hat and use a high-factor sunscreen.

Drugs
You have the choice of pharmacies dispensing western medicines or 'Chinese medical halls' selling traditional Chinese herbal medicines. They are often found in department stores and supermarkets and are well stocked for minor ailments.

Safe Water
It is quite safe to drink tap water in major cities in Peninsular Malaysia. In other areas water may be contaminated, especially during the monsoon season, and should be boiled. Bottled water is widely available. Remember to drink enough!

CONCESSIONS

Students/Youths Malaysia is appealing for youth and student travel because of its low cost of living and wide range of outdoor activities. Student and youth discounts are mostly confined to Malaysian nationals. An International Student Identity Card (ISIC) is of limited use but worth bringing as it can be useful at hostels; flashing it may sometimes bring discounts.
Senior Citizens Malaysia is not an obvious destination for older travellers, some find the equatorial climate difficult to cope with. There are, however, holidays specifically designed for senior citizens such as those offered by Saga Holidays, Saga Building, Middelburg Square, Folkestone, Kent CT20 1AZ, United Kingdom (☎ 0800 414383).

CLOTHING SIZES

Malaysia	UK	Rest of Europe	USA	
36	36	46	36	
38	38	48	38	
40	40	50	40	Suits
42	42	52	42	
44	44	54	44	
46	46	56	46	
7	7	41	8	
7.5	7.5	42	8.5	
8.5	8.5	43	9.5	Shoes
9.5	9.5	44	10.5	
10.5	10.5	45	11.5	
11	11	46	12	
14.5	14.5	37	14.5	
15	15	38	15	
15.5	15.5	39/40	15.5	Shirts
16	16	41	16	
16.5	16.5	42	16.5	
17	17	43	17	
8	8	34	6	
10	10	36	8	
12	12	38	10	Dresses
14	14	40	12	
16	16	42	14	
18	18	44	16	
4.5	4.5	38	6	
5	5	38	6.5	
5.5	5.5	39	7	Shoes
6	6	39	7.5	
6.5	6.5	40	8	
7	7	41	8.5	

WHEN DEPARTING

- On your arrival in Malaysia you complete a disembarkation form; the embarkation portion returned to you must be presented on your departure.
- There is an airport departure tax of RM40 for international flights and RM5 for domestic flights payable at airline check-in desks.

LANGUAGE

Bahasa Malaysia is the official language of Malaysia, but as it is a multi-racial country you will hear many languages. Bahasa Malaysia is a colourful mixture of many other tongues – including Sanskrit, Arabic and English. English is very widely spoken. People in former British Borneo are fluent English-speakers and most Kuala Lumpur taxi drivers know some words. Below are some words of Bahasa Malaysia you may find helpful.

hotel	*hotel*	fan	*kipas angin*
rest house	*rumah rehat*	hot water	*air panas*
lodging house	*rumah tumpangan*	bathroom	*bilik mandi*
room	*bilik*	toilet	*tandas*
..for one/two people	*..untuk satu/dua orang*	bed	*tempat tidur*
		bed sheet	*cadar*
..for one/two nights	*..untuk satu/dua malam*	pillow	*bantal*
		sleep	*tidur*
air-conditioning	*air-con-kah*	telephone	*telepon*

bank	*bank*	coin	*duit/wang syiling*
exchange office	*penukar matawang*	credit card	*kad kredit*
		traveller's cheque	*cek kembara*
post office	*pejat pos*	exchange rate	*kadar tukaran asing*
foreign exchange	*tukaran matawang asing*		
		commission charge	*cas kamisyen*
money	*wang/duit*		
dollar	*ringgit*	how much?	*berapa harganya?*
cent	*sen*	expensive	*mahal*
banknote	*duit/wang kerlas*	cheap	*murah*

restaurant	*restoran*	vegetables	*sayur-sayuran*
soup	*sup*	boiled rice	*nasi putih*
beef	*daging lembu*	fried rice	*nasi goreng*
pork	*babi*	fried noodles	*mee goreng*
chicken	*ayam*	hot (spicy)	*pedas*
fish	*ikan*	sweet (tasting)	*manis*
prawns	*udang*	cold	*sejuk*
egg	*telur*	drinks	*minuman*

aeroplane	*kapal terbang*	taxi	*teksi*
airport	*lapangan terbang*	car	*kereta*
train	*keretapi*	rickshaw/trishaw	*beca*
..station	*..stesen keretapi*	ticket	*tiket*
bus	*bas*	..single/return	*..satu hala/pergi balik*
..station	*..stesen bas*		
boat	*perahu/bot*	..first/second class	*..kelas satu*
..port	*..pelabuhan*	.. economy class	*..kelas ekonomi*

yes	*ya*	sorry	*saya minta maaf*
no	*tidak*	excuse me	*maafkan saya*
please	*tolong/silakan*	help!	*tolong!*
thank you	*terima kasih*	today	*hari ini*
hello	*hello/apa khabar*	tomorrow	*besok*
good morning	*selamat pagi*	yesterday	*kelmarin*
goodnight	*selamat malam*	open	*buka*
goodbye	*selamat tinggal*	closed	*tutup*

INDEX

Acknowledgements
The Automobile Assocation wishes to thank the following photographers and libraries for their assistance in the preparation of this book:
BRUCE COLEMAN COLLECTION 65; FIONA DUNLOP 86, 87, 88, 88/9, 90; FOOTPRINTS 22/3 (Nick Hanna), 77 and 84 (P Waldock); GETTY IMAGES 14; JAMES DAVIS F/cover (b): Kuantan, Chempedak Beach; MALAYSIA TOURISM PROMOTION BOARD 9a; MARY EVANS PICTURE LIBRARY 10, 11; MRI BANKERS'S GUIDE TO FOREIGN CURRENCY 119; NATURE PHOTOGRAPHERS LTD 66a, 66b and 66c (J Sutherland); PICTURES F/cover (c): young girl; SPECTRUM COLOUR LIBRARY 83.

The remaining photographs are held in the Association's own library (**AA PHOTO LIBRARY**) and were taken by N Hanna 1, 6a, 6b, 15b, 17, 19, 21, 45, 72, 75, 78, 79; K Paterson F/cover (a): Pulau Kapas, F/cover (d); Cheong Patt Tze Masio, B/cover: cakes, 2, 5a, 7, 8a, 8b, 8c, 12/13, 15a, 16, 18, 20, 23a, 24, 25, 26, 27a, 27b, 28/9, 30, 31, 34, 35, 36, 37, 38, 39, 41, 42, 43, 44, 46, 47, 48, 49, 50, 51, 52, 53, 54/5, 56, 57, 58, 59, 60, 61, 62, 63, 64, 67, 68/9, 70, 71, 73, 80, 81a, 81b, 91b, 117a, 117b.

Contributors
Copy editor: Nia Williams   **Page Layout:** The Company of Designers   **Verifier:** Polly Phillimore
Researcher (Practical Matters): Colin Follett   **Indexer:** Marie Lorimer

Dear Essential Traveller

**Your comments, opinions and recommendations are very
important to us. So please help us to improve our travel
guides by taking a few minutes to complete this simple
questionnaire.**

*You do not need a stamp (unless posted outside the UK). If you do not want to cut this page
from your guide, then photocopy it or write your answers on a plain sheet of paper.*

Send to: **The Editor, AA World Travel Guides,
FREEPOST SCE 4598, Basingstoke RG21 4GY.**

Your recommendations...

We always encourage readers' recommendations for restaurants, nightlife
or shopping – if your recommendation is used in the next edition of the
guide, we will send you a *FREE* AA *Essential* **Guide** of your choice.
Please state below the establishment name, location and your reasons
for recommending it.

_____

_____

_____

_____

Please send me **AA *Essential*** _____
(*see list of titles inside the front cover*)

About this guide...

Which title did you buy?
   AA *Essential* _____
Where did you buy it? _____
When? m m / y y

Why did you choose an AA *Essential* Guide? _____

_____

_____

_____

_____

Did this guide meet your expectations?
   Exceeded ☐ Met all ☐ Met most ☐ Fell below ☐
   Please give your reasons_____

_____

_____

_____

continued on next page...

Were there any aspects of this guide that you particularly liked? _____

_____

_____

_____

Is there anything we could have done better? _____

_____

_____

_____

_____

About you…

Name (*Mr/Mrs/Ms*) _____

    Address _____

_____

_____ Postcode _____

    Daytime tel nos _____

Which age group are you in?
  Under 25 ☐ 25–34 ☐ 35–44 ☐ 45–54 ☐ 55–64 ☐ 65+ ☐

How many trips do you make a year?
  Less than one ☐ One ☐ Two ☐ Three or more ☐

Are you an AA member? Yes ☐ No ☐

About your trip…

When did you book? m m / y y   When did you travel? m m / y y

How long did you stay? _____

Was it for business or leisure? _____

Did you buy any other travel guides for your trip?

    If yes, which ones? _____

_____

Thank you for taking the time to complete this questionnaire. Please send
it to us as soon as possible, and remember, you do not need a stamp
(*unless posted outside the UK*).

Happy Holidays!